Guidelines

KW-334-407

VOL 27 / PART 1
January–April 2011

Commissioned by **Jeremy Duff**; *edited by* **Lisa Cherrett**

Guidelines © BRF 2011
The Bible Reading Fellowship
15 The Chambers, Vineyard, Abingdon OX14 3FE
Tel: 01865 319700; Fax: 01865 319701
E-mail: enquiries@brf.org.uk; Website: www.brf.org.uk

ISBN 978 1 84101 627 6

Distributed in Australia by Willow Connection, PO Box 288, Brookvale, NSW 2100.
Tel: 02 9948 3957; Fax: 02 9948 8153;
E-mail: info@willowconnection.com.au
Available also from all good Christian bookshops in Australia.
For individual and group subscriptions in Australia:
Mrs Rosemary Morrall, PO Box W35, Wanniassa, ACT 2903.

Distributed in New Zealand by Scripture Union Wholesale, PO Box 760, Wellington
Tel: 04 385 0421; Fax: 04 384 3990; E-mail: suwholesale@clear.net.nz

Publications distributed to more than 60 countries

Acknowledgments
The New Revised Standard Version of the Bible, Anglicized Edition, copyright © 1989, 1995 by the
Division of Christian Education of the National Council of the Churches of Christ in the USA. Used
by permission. All rights reserved.

The Holy Bible, New International Version, copyright © 1973, 1978, 1984, 1995 by International Bible
Society. Used by permission of Hodder & Stoughton Publishers, a member of the Hachette Livre
UK Group. All rights reserved. 'NIV' is a registered trademark of International Bible Society. UK
trademark number 1448790.

The Holy Bible, Today's New International Version, copyright © 2004 by International Bible Society.
Used by permission of Hodder & Stoughton Publishers, a member of the Hachette Livre UK Group.
All rights reserved. 'TNIV' is a registered trademark of International Bible Society.

The New Jerusalem Bible, published and copyright © 1985 by Darton, Longman and Todd Ltd and
les Editions du Cerf, and by Doubleday, a division of Bantam Doubleday Dell Publishing Group,
Inc. Used by permission of Darton, Longman and Todd Ltd, and Doubleday, a division of Random
house, Inc.

Extracts from the Authorised Version of the Bible (The King James Bible), the rights in which are
vested in the Crown, are reproduced by permission of the Crown's Patentee, Cambridge University
Press.

Revised Grail Psalms copyright © 2008, Conception Abbey/The Grail, admin. by GIA Publications,
Inc., www.giamusic.com. All rights reserved.

'One more step along the world I go' by Sydney Carter (1915–2004). Copyright © 1971 Stainer &
Bell Ltd, London, England: www.stainer.co.uk

Printed in Singapore by Craft Print International Ltd

Suggestions for using *Guidelines*

Set aside a regular time and place, if possible, when you can read and pray undisturbed. Before you begin, take time to be still and, if you find it helpful, use the BRF prayer.

In *Guidelines*, the introductory section provides context for the passages or themes to be studied, while the units of comment can be used daily, weekly, or whatever best fits your timetable. You will need a Bible (more than one if you want to compare different translations) as Bible passages are not included. At the end of each week is a 'Guidelines' section, offering further thoughts about, or practical application of what you have been studying.

You may find it helpful to keep a journal to record your thoughts about your study, or to note items for prayer. Another way of using *Guidelines* is to meet with others to discuss the material, either regularly or occasionally.

Occasionally, you may read something in *Guidelines* that you find particularly challenging, even uncomfortable. This is inevitable in a series of notes which draws on a wide spectrum of contributors, and doesn't believe in ducking difficult issues. Indeed, we believe that *Guidelines* readers much prefer thought-provoking material to a bland diet that only confirms what they already think.

If you do disagree with a contributor, you may find it helpful to go through these three steps. First, think about why you feel uncomfortable. Perhaps this is an idea that is new to you, or you are not happy at the way something has been expressed. Or there may be something more substantial—you may feel that the writer is guilty of sweeping generalisation, factual error, theological or ethical misjudgment. Second, pray that God would use this disagreement to teach you more about his word and about yourself. Third, think about what you will do as a result of the disagreement. You might resolve to find out more about the issue, or write to the contributor or the editors of *Guidelines*. After all, we aim to be 'doers of the word', not just people who hold opinions about it.

Writers in this issue

Alec Gilmore is a Baptist minister, author, lecturer and Senior Research Fellow at the International Baptist Theological Seminary, Prague. His most recent book is *A Concise Dictionary of Bible Origins and Interpretation* (T&T Clark/Continuum, 2007)

Joanna Collicutt, an Anglican priest, is Senior Lecturer in Psychology of Religion at Heythrop College. Previously she worked as a consultant clinical psychologist, specialising in the needs of people with complex disabilities. She has a particular interest in psychological approaches to Bible reading.

Amy Orr-Ewing is Training Director for the Zacharias Trust and is involved in evangelism, apologetics and teaching both in the UK and abroad. She is a lecturer at the Oxford Centre for Apologetics, Wycliffe Hall, and lives in London with her husband and three boys.

Peter Walker is Associate Vice-Principal and Director of Development at Wycliffe Hall, Oxford, where he lectures in New Testament Studies and Biblical Theology. He has a special interest in the historical Jesus. As a qualified tour guide around Israel, he leads student groups on tours every other year.

Henry Wansbrough OSB is a monk at Ampleforth Abbey in Yorkshire. He is Executive Secretary of the International Commission for Producing an English-Language Lectionary (ICPEL) for the Roman Catholic Church, and lectures frequently across the globe.

Jeremy Duff is a vicar in Widnes with a teaching and writing ministry, which has included posts at Liverpool Cathedral and within Oxford University. His writings include *Meeting Jesus: Human Responses to a Yearning God* (SPCK, 2006) and *The Elements of New Testament Greek* (CUP, 2005).

Tom Wilson is currently Curate to the Toxteth Team, a group of three churches in inner-city Liverpool. He also teaches Biblical Studies for the Regional Training Partnership. He enjoys teaching, training and helping people to develop their gifts and deepen their relationship with Jesus.

Lisa Cherrett has worked for BRF since 1997 as Project Editor and, in more recent years, as Managing Editor for the Bible reading notes. She is a member of the lay ministry team at her local Baptist church.

Janet Fletcher is a priest at Prescot in Liverpool Diocese, and coordinator of the Diocesan Spiritual Director Training Course. She offers spiritual direction and quiet days, and leads courses on prayer and spirituality. She has written *Pathway to God: Following the Way in Prayer* (SPCK, 2006).

The Editor writes...

Real life—life with all its inner questioning, hopes, anxieties, problems and dreams—is at the heart of this edition of *Guidelines*. God is concerned for the realities of our lives. Indeed, he came and entered into real human life in all its confusions and turmoil, and has given us a Bible shot through with the reality of life, not a 'stained-glass window', sanitised version.

We begin with Genesis 12—24 (the story of Abraham), which Alec Gilmore compares to a soap opera, full of the drama and eccentricities of real life, inviting us to find God in the story of our life. Then Joanna Collicutt McGrath guides us through 'Luke's strange and sacred journeys', highlighting for us a feature of Luke and Acts—that our Christian life is portrayed as a journey, during which (not just at the end) we encounter God. Next we face full-on the questions that are asked of our faith, in Amy Orr-Ewing's notes on Apologetics. These notes aim to help us answer not only the questions of others, but also our own.

The Gospel for this year is Matthew, which we pick up at the halfway point. Peter Walker leads us through Matthew 15—20, in which Jesus is bombarded with questions but through which we are challenged to examine our own hearts in all their complexity. Our Psalms (with Henry Wansbrough) for this edition are 26—37, some of the most intense and personal in the whole Psalter, encompassing the high and lows, the joy and despair of life. Jeremy Duff then guides us through Hebrews, one of the richest, densest and most pastorally meaningful books of the Bible, whose author repeatedly both encourages and challenges his readers in their daily lives.

Then we have two short contributions, each focusing on a different aspect of life. First, Tom Wilson opens up for us the issue of 'Success', then Lisa Cherrett considers 'Finding peace of mind'. These are both issues at the heart of our human existence, and about which, as Tom and Lisa demonstrate, the Bible has much to offer. Finally for this issue, Janet Fletcher leads us in a meditation on Holy Week to Easter, drawing out that 'love was his meaning'. It is fitting to end our wrestles with the complexity of human life with this reminder of the all-encompassing, sacrificial love of God.

Jeremy Duff
Commissioning Editor

The BRF Prayer

Almighty God,
you have taught us that your word is a lamp for our
feet and a light for our path. Help us, and all who
prayerfully read your word, to deepen our
fellowship with each other through your love. And
in so doing may we come to know you more fully,
love you more truly, and follow more faithfully in
the steps of your son Jesus Christ, who lives and
reigns with you and the Holy Spirit,
one God for evermore. Amen.

Genesis 12—24: Abraham for today

Try reading these early narratives as stories of human life, not unlike soap opera. Of their origins there is scant evidence. A widespread view among scholars is that, in their present form, they come from a much later time than the events they describe. They derive from memories of ancestral figures, handed down for generations, edited and preserved by Israelites who saw their significance for their own situation, possibly a thousand years later. This gives us a mandate to explore their value for our lives rather than agonising over their history, authenticity or morality.

Like soap operas, these are rattling good stories, deserving of a wide audience, even if they often have an air of unreality. They describe incidents that could 'never happen' in real life (though we should bear in mind that TV soap is based on true experience and often, after watching even one of the more outlandish episodes, we can run across similar real-life stories within weeks). The language, especially the way they talk about God, may not be the language of your friends and contemporaries, but that is no reason either for rejecting the stories or for imitating the language in order to appreciate the experience.

Despite the differences and eccentricities, the world of soap reveals itself as a cross-section of the world we live in. There is love and care, selfishness and sacrifice, inequalities (some chosen, some not), suffering and hardship, friendship and loneliness, pleasure, frustration and satisfaction—but always with a forward-looking approach, the participants never knowing what will happen next but having a positive interest in the discovery. It offers not just something to see, read or study, but an invitation to get involved.

When we get involved in these stories from Genesis, we often find that it is a short step to 'the Word made flesh' (John 1:14). They provide the key to a better understanding of what God is doing where we are. There are also side-effects: food for thought about things we take for granted, issues we might otherwise be unaware of, and a totally different (if somewhat exaggerated) view of life.

This is one of many ways to find God in the story of our life. What is he doing? What can we expect from him? What does he expect from us? How do we hear his voice and relate to him?

1 Get up and go

Genesis 12:1–9

Soap begins by introducing its characters, so we begin with Abram. Try to spot experiences in this story where you can identify with him.

Here is a man with a deep urge to get up and go. Out there was something to be grasped but it was not going to come to him. He had to go and get it. He had no idea what hazards he might encounter, no certainty that he would find what he was looking for, no reason to believe he would recognise the place when he got there, and no rational answer to give if his friends asked 'where?' or 'why?' Of his understanding of God, we know nothing. All we can say with certainty is that it was very different from ours, but, if pressed, he would say, 'God told me to'.

That may not be your experience—or is it? Read it simply as a story of new beginnings, possibly relating it to a moment in your life when, for whatever reason, you had to begin all over again. What were your emotions?

What else have you got in common with Abram? His age seems not to have entered into the question of whether to make this new start. His family (Sarai and Lot), apparently, were not consulted. Relations with Lot subsequently were not all sweetness and light: he might have predicted that taking Lot with him could bring problems, but he seems not to have thought of that. It was simply one of those things he knew he had to do. Even more surprisingly, he sees the whole operation as an investment for his offspring (v. 7), which he hasn't got and seems unlikely to have.

Like many a soap, the story is crazy. It surely can't run. Nobody lives like that. But they do, and the story has run for 4000 years. Why? Abram did what he did because he felt strongly about something. He even held God responsible for the conviction, and that is what gave him hope. Like one who came later, he knew that if he wanted to live, he had to begin with a readiness to die and begin again.

If this is still not your experience, go back to a more fundamental question. What is your story? Where are you going, and why?

2 Family problems

Genesis 13:1–13

Every soap has its family quarrels, and family members who don't like a quarrel usually spend time trying to avoid one. Abram's family was no exception but, since this is a very early episode in our story, it is worth asking what might have happened before, that we have not seen. What might be the 'back-story'?

If you have ever lived or worked where one person had a natural position of power and a strong conviction of some sort, you would have no difficulty writing one or two 'previous' episodes. You may well feel, 'I know a man like that', so ask a few questions. Whom did Abram consult before the move? Sarah? Presumably not: she was a woman. The herdsmen? Almost certainly not: workers would do what they were told. Lot? Maybe yes, maybe no. But if Abram consulted nobody, small wonder he soon ran into difficulties. When the trouble came, it was not the fault of the family so much as the inadequate resources. The land could not provide sufficient for all their needs (v. 6) and, although the heart of the family seemed able to cope, the situation was intolerable to the point of strife for the workers.

By now you may be thinking of something similar in a different situation. Stay with it. Is the threat of limited resources real or imaginary? Is someone using it for their own advantage?

Abram's offer seems a generous one. He gives Lot the choice. Lot's decision tells us a lot about his character, and the narrator puts the boot in by adding verse 13, possibly as a preparation for what is to follow. In view of Abram's strong conviction, though, it is strange that he seems never even to have shared the problem with God. How can he allow Lot to decide what God has given him and just expect God to go along with it?

This story says a lot about the way we relate to one another, the pressures we live under, the choices we make, the way we handle strong convictions when it comes to the crunch, and the way we take God for granted when it suits our purposes.

3 A fresh start

Genesis 15:1–6, 17–18

By this episode, Abram has revealed some very human characteristics: doubt, uncertainty, anxiety, a desire to see into the future and a desire for children. To these he adds impatience.

Think of a situation in which you might feel a strong urge to take a new and bold step—perhaps in a relationship, job, hobby, sport or project. You lack nothing in determination and enthusiasm. If asked for reasons, you have them ready. If cautioned, you can handle other people's reservations. This is something you have to do; you can, and you will. In certain circles, you might even say, 'I know this is what God is telling me to do', and to that there is no answer. But then, how many times do you hear that whisper of doubt coming over your shoulder—when something goes wrong, someone lets you down, you feel weary, or the plan just isn't working out, at least not quite as you had hoped?

That is where Abram stands. He has been obliged to appoint his own servant, Eleazar, as his heir. Surely this is not what God intended—or, if it is, Abram has been seriously misled. His clear expectation was for a son with Sarai, but the biological clock is ticking and nothing is happening. Confidence is cracking. This time he does consult God and receives substantial reassurance, the promise of an heir being enhanced with the addition of land and a new covenant (v. 18).

But it is still all talk, dreams and promises. Talk is easy. The fulfilment of promises depends on all kinds of responses from others as well as from Abram himself. Some occasions call for patience, and Abram has not yet come to terms with God's timing. Faith may teach us that God always keeps his promises, but it does not always tell us that God's promise might not be exactly what we thought it was, and the fulfilment does not necessarily come when we think it should.

This is the moment when faith is tested. We have to learn patience, which sometimes requires us to hang on until another urge tells us differently or corrects our direction. That, too, can be the voice of God.

4 New name, new boundaries

Genesis 17:1–14

Continued faithfulness is rewarded by renewed recognition, new names and a reaffirmation of the covenant. A new school calls for a new uniform, a new business for a new logo; so we now have a new Hebrew name for God (El-Shaddai; 'Elohim' is used previously) and changes for Abraham and Sarah, though their significance is uncertain. What we still need to remember is that we cannot attribute to this God (of whatever name) all that we today associate with the God of Moses and the prophets (Yahweh), and God as revealed in Jesus. When we think of God, our concepts are quite different from those of the Jews, and Jewish concepts are different from those of the patriarchs.

Recall your own experience of fresh starts, changed names and new logos. Were they cosmetic or did they reflect real change, and, if the latter, change for whom?

Change in this story seems to suggest a broadening of the horizon. Abraham is now promised 'a multitude of nations' (v. 4), fruitfulness beyond measure, parity with neighbouring kings, firm land tenure and a secure future. Such is the way new starts are made. In contemporary terms, this is electioneering with a vengeance: everything promised, no guarantee and no delivery date. But now there are also conditions placed on Abraham and his descendants. One is obedience. Failure to keep the covenant will result in a loss of privileges and will nullify any special relationship (v. 14). So with a broadening of horizons comes a narrowing of focus.

Circumcision is the new initiation ceremony (or logo), but is this mark of belonging intended to confirm the status of those who are 'in' or to make abundantly clear who is not? Once again, as the boundaries get wider, the entrance gates seem to become more restricted.

With the date of the texts uncertain, and allowing for frequent editorial changes, it is not clear whether the new names for Abraham and Sarah are really new (signifying a fresh start) or whether they are a reading back into an earlier story of something that emerged much later, possibly when Jews were wrestling with the problem of whether Judaism was a missionary faith with a God who embraced all peoples (as in Ruth, Esther and Daniel) or an exclusive group with a God who worked only for them (Ezra, Nehemiah and Jonah). Circumcision may have marked a boundary, but did it become a passport? The resolution is not easy and there is no definitive answer. The questions are still with us.

5 Running away

Genesis 16

This is the first episode in a two-part story. Begin with a few simple questions. Who is the hero? Who is the villain? With whom do you have most empathy? Who comes out best, and who worst? Traditionally, it is a story of the still childless Abram, Sarai's attempt to solve the problem and a slave woman, Hagar, rejected when no longer needed—but there may be more to it.

Phyllis Trible, for example, asks how this could ever be seen as a story about Abraham. It is a story of two women: Sarah (power) and Hagar (powerlessness), and, since Hagar is the first woman in scripture to receive a divine visit and the first to receive an annunciation, she suggests that it is a story of Hagar (and Sarah) rather than Sarah (and Hagar). We could think of Hagar as the 'suffering servant' (Isaiah 53) or maybe the forerunner of the 'stone that the builders rejected' (Acts 4:11).

When three groups of middle-to-upper-class Catholic and Protestant women were asked to 'identify Hagar', there were four different answers. Privileged but barren women in North California saw Hagar as an accomplice, a fixer and an opportunist. Divorced and rejected women in the same group saw her as an outcast. Refugees and exiles from Mexico and Central America—women who were displaced, unwanted, isolated from family and friends and all things familiar, who knew what it was like to run away and were still looking for an escape—saw her as an exile whom God did not liberate but for whom he provided the means for survival. Black South Africans, who had grown up under apartheid, saw her as an Egyptian slave and an exploited worker.

In three of these four views, Hagar was a victim. Isolated and living in the desert, she hears a voice, and responds with the words, 'Surely this is a place where I, in my turn, have seen the one who sees me' (v. 13, Jerusalem Bible). What makes the difference, says Trevor Dennis (in *The Book of*

Books), is not Hagar 'seeing God' but her realisation that God has seen her. She goes back, but with a new name for God: 'the God who sees'.

6 Life in the wilderness

Genesis 21:8–20

In the second episode of the two-parter, time has moved on. Isaac has arrived. Ishmael, his older half-brother, is playing. Sarah has never come to terms with her jealousy. Not satisfied that she has got what she wanted, having once tried to remove her own competition she now has to remove Isaac's. Last time, Hagar ran away. This time, she is banished with no hope of return.

Praying for those who experience what Hagar experienced is tough and painful. Think of someone whose life has been completely turned upside down and can never be the same again, as a result of something for which they were only partly responsible. Then, once they made a recovery and were getting back to normal, they found themselves taken over by forces totally beyond their control and plunged into a second wilderness even worse than the first. That man, woman or child knows something of the wilderness in which Hagar found herself. Or think of nations or races once invaded and occupied and then, having achieved independence, finding themselves ostracised because, from time to time, what they do displeases others who hold power.

Hagar has many children: victims of apartheid in South Africa, the Aborigines in Australia and the North American Indians, all now grown up but still suffering as, only slowly, we become more aware of their plight and feel the need to say sorry. There are also many groups in our own society that we might think of. The story of Hagar and her children is a story about power—the price of power and who pays it.

How, then, do we find God in such situations? Perhaps we find him when we discover that 'the God who sees' is also 'the God who hears'. He hears the weeping, but, if the child is to be saved, Hagar must play her part. She is not to abandon Ishmael but to come near, lift him up and hold him tight. When she does, God opens her eyes and she sees the water in the well. It was there all the time, but she only saw it when she held Ishmael tight. So (says Trevor Dennis), 'the God who sees' and 'the God who hears' becomes 'the God who saves'.

Guidelines

- Try drafting a few paragraphs about what might have been happening before the story of Abram began, or what you would expect to happen in the episode after Hagar returns to the fold.
- How do you decide when to consult God and on what issues, and how and when do you carry on without consultation?
- Are we at a point where we have to rethink our understanding of monotheism, and, if we reaffirm it, do we have to reconsider how we understand the one God? We may no longer want to claim God as Catholic, Protestant or Orthodox, but are we ready to broaden our horizons further, and are our rites and ceremonies essentially food for the faithful or signs of exclusivity?

1 Childlessness

Genesis 18:1–15

Babies are the stock-in-trade of soap opera. For Abraham and Sarah, the biological clock had stopped ticking. The problem of childlessness—including the shame, embarrassment or sense of failure that often goes with it—seems very familiar.

This is probably not a story for those who are currently facing childlessness, since it underlines the tragedy of the situation and the fact that, in the last resort, it is beyond our control. The story does, however, have a positive message, which says that we should be determined to do all we possibly can and never lose hope, while always recognising that what works for one does not necessarily work for all. If it still doesn't work, we should try not to be resentful but can turn elsewhere (including the scriptures) for reassurance and consolation.

Verses 9–15 seem a strange insertion. They tell us nothing that we have not been told before; they raise unhelpful questions about who these strangers were and how they could be so confident that Sarah would have a son; and, although the incident seems to lead into what follows, it has no direct connection with it. Could we be missing something? Let us stick to what we know.

Three strangers turn up on the doorstep and Abraham gives them the customary Eastern hospitality. Since they arrived 'in the heat of the day' (v. 1) and stayed the night, what did they talk about? Given Abraham's obsession with his covenant and promise, it would be surprising if he didn't share it with them, and, with the clear absence of any offspring, the subject of his childlessness would inevitably arise. Sarah is in the tent, either eavesdropping or overhearing, but 'laughs to herself' at the thought of bearing a son (v. 12). She and Abraham have gone through this so many times before. Sarah: 'It isn't going to happen.' Abraham: 'Oh yes, it is.' Next morning, the strangers leave with words of encouragement, which keep the story alive and the narrative moving on.

Couples who struggle with childlessness need that sympathetic ear to keep hope alive—understanding without interference (found often in unlikely places and sometimes most helpfully from strangers)—while all the time keeping their feet on the ground. Maybe you hear somebody calling.

2 A question of justice

Genesis 18:16–33

The strangers journey on to Sodom and Gomorrah, two cities of much alleged depravity on the plain of Jordan. Abraham, ever attentive to the voice of God, knows that if they find what they expect to find, those cities will be destroyed. He is also aware that, somewhere down there, he has a nephew with a family business. In essentials, this story provides a backdrop to our world, and it is not difficult to move in imagination from the one to the other.

Think of any group of people going about their daily business. Some aspect of their behaviour may be right or wrong in their own eyes, and may incur suspicion, horror or fear in others who otherwise are unaffected by them. One day, along come a few of the 'others', who share their concern with you and tell you that they are on their way to check whether what they have heard is true. If it is, they plan to put a stop to that behaviour, whatever it takes.

What do you do? They may be right, but do you interfere? There is probably nothing you can do. You are just one against three, and they seem pretty determined. There's no point even asking questions—and apparently Abraham doesn't. You could hardly be blamed if you came to the same conclusion. But then you realise that these strangers are on the warpath to a place where you have family, and suddenly you are standing exactly where Abraham stood.

Abraham does the only thing he can do: he talks to God. How many innocent people have to be sacrificed in order to root out a few who displease? Fifty? Forty? Thirty? Ten? 'Shall not the Judge of all the earth do what is just'? (v. 25).

In this way, Abraham takes one step further in understanding his relationship with God. The first step was in Haran (obedience), the next in his dealings with Hagar (compassion), Isaac (reliability) and now Lot (justice). Incidents like this—not so much the Bible stories as the contemporary events that they bring into focus—constantly challenge us to go through the same exercise. What we have believed until now may be fine, but life is a constant challenge, not only in matters of justice. Like Abraham, we grow in faith only to the extent that we grow in our understanding of God.

3 The remnant

Genesis 19:1–26

In all soaps, some episodes defy understanding and rationality. This may be one such.

What Lot offers his visitors is the basic level of hospitality in his culture (vv. 1–3). Abraham did as much the day before (18:1–8). We may be horrified by Lot's offer of his two daughters to the mob (v. 8) but in all stories (soaps especially) we have to judge people by their own societies and backgrounds, rather than our own. In Lot's culture, hospitality overrides all other considerations. We are on firmer ground if we stick to the point that any society, when confronted by unwelcome visitors intent on destruction, whoever they are and wherever they are from, knows that there is usually a price to be paid by someone.

The fact that all the men are specifically said to have been involved (v. 4) may suggest a macho-unanimity, if not a wild mob with the bit between their teeth, and may leave some readers wondering how different it might be today in some places. Others may prefer to reflect on the idea that, since the whole is more than the sum of the parts, so also the power of any collective (race, mob or nation state) may lead people to behave in a way that, as individuals, they would never contemplate.

We have no idea what actually brought about the destruction of the two cities, and no historical basis can be found for the story. If you see it as a natural disaster, such as an earthquake (as has been suggested), that could lead to some theological questions about our understanding of God.

If we focus on Abraham, it is not difficult to see how subsequent generations warmed to the story. It enhanced their 'father figure', developed the story, eliminated what did not fit and so ensured their own place as God's people from the very beginning and at every stage on the journey. His preservation also has within it the seeds of 'a remnant'—a concept of the faithful that the Jews found helpful many years later, when it seemed as if the world was collapsing around them.

For Lot and his family, it suggests the importance of knowing when to move on and when not to look back!

4 Threat to life

Genesis 22:1–13

In the Christian tradition, the stature of Abraham as the very epitome of faith and faithfulness (Hebrews 11:8–12, 17–19; James 2:21) is solid and unquestioned. Scholars Gunn and Fewell, however, point out that there are times when he appears hesitant and uncertain, long on dreams and hopes but short on what is going on around him. He is the powerful head of a family from which he is somewhat detached, in need of constant confidence-boosting. Now comes the biggest test of all.

Abraham's journey had never been trouble-free. Driven by his enormous conviction and never looking back, he had pursued his quest for a new home and a family—children, grandchildren and great-grandchildren, with himself at the pinnacle—yet with Sarah he couldn't even manage one child.

Then it happened: a son, in old age. With that, followed by a deal with Abimelech (21:22–24), things began to look up. Now he really was on course for the promised land. But then (as always in soaps), when the sun comes out, disaster soon strikes. The God who promised all of this tells him to break it up. Isaac must be sacrificed.

Why? Was the dream false? Did Abraham get it wrong? Is God testing him or is he testing God? Perhaps he is gambling all to prove himself to family and friends, to God or to himself. Or is the old tradition of sacrificing what is most pure and precious as a demonstration of conviction—not unknown among the surrounding nations with which he grew up—coming into conflict with the new (new beginning, new name, new ethic)? Whatever it is, this insecure and uncertain 'man of faith' is on trial once again.

At first, he has no doubt. The old holds sway: the boy must go. The new must find its own way of breaking through and, no doubt, will. That really is faith. The day arrives. The deed must be done. Right to the wire we go before the new reclaims control. An alternative presents itself, a reason is found, the plan is changed, and the sun shines again. This really is a new beginning, but only just.

How different Jewish and Christian history would have been if Abraham had got it wrong!

5 Sarah's obituary

Genesis 23:1–15

Some things change little in 4000 years. Where we bury our dead is crucial. Land is important and Abraham, an alien in a foreign land, doesn't have any, but such is the way the Hittites treat aliens that he is offered 'the choicest of our burial places' (v. 6) as a gift. The details are uncertain. The story may come from the time when Jews were re-establishing themselves after the exile, anxious to stress that that land was the fulfilment of God's promise. It gave them a right, and it gave them hope.

For us, it says something about our common humanity and the needs of aliens, but also about Sarah. Many of us get more recognition in death than in life, and Sarah is no exception. We are even told that Abraham, detached and insecure though he may have been, mourned and wept for her (v. 2). Deaths call for reflection and appreciation, and obituaries have their own way of helping us to see people differently. If you were to write Sarah's obituary, what would you say?

You might say that living with Abraham could never have been easy. Did she ever regret offering Hagar to him? Was she simply following custom? Did she feel boxed in? How did she decide between wanting and surrendering? Or was it a generous gesture, made out of love for her husband and his future? Perhaps she had a big heart but lacked the stamina and spiritual resources to go through with the consequences—which would explain why her only solution was to banish both Hagar and Ishmael.

Think, too, about Abraham and Sarah's relationship before and after the incident with Hagar. Did she go to Abraham for help and support, or was she simply doing what she knew she had to do? Did she get the response she wanted, or expected, or knew she had to accept? Some people might feel she was every bit as much a victim of circumstances as Hagar was.

Never mind the different culture. The issue is not in the historic details but in the pressures that all societies and families force upon their members.

6 Marriage and the succession

Genesis 24:10–15, 45–51

Act 1 comes to an end with an elderly widower, an heir who has survived and the need of a wife for that heir, to take the story on. A servant is despatched to find one.

If the method seems somewhat bizarre (vv. 13–14), remember both that this is an arranged marriage and that, in any story, it is common for a whole series of events to be reduced to a single line ('I knew at the time she was the right one because of her care for the camels'). What often sounds unbelievable in a love story (or a soap) is often not as crazy as it seems, and the summary statement in verses 50–51 is not all that different from the words of someone who says, 'I prayed about it and God gave me his answer.' The essence is familiar to us.

Not every story, of course, has such a happy ending. No doubt Rebekah had many friends who could tell a different story. If you feel that there is too strong an air of unreality, though, that may be partly due to the way the story is told. Laban's remark in verse 50 is still to be heard, even if it slips too readily off the tongue in some circles and is meaningless to others. If truth is stranger than fiction, it is worth remembering that there are times when we can see no other solution or explanation for what happens. There are also times when we need to be open to the miraculous, and other situations when we need to acknowledge that 'God knows best', even if we would not choose to put it that way. Perhaps you can think of some examples.

In this case, it is easy to say 'Amen' to Laban's comment, but that is only because we know the end of the story. For Laban, as indeed for Abraham throughout, this was not a judgment after the event, but an act of faith before it took place. It marks a new stage in the story of the promise. Abraham's heir has not only survived but he also has an eminently suitable wife, destined to produce another heir, the inheritor of the promise in the third generation. Here we see 'the continual guidance of God at every stage' (R.N. Whybray).

Guidelines

- Without getting involved in the claims of Abraham or Jewish politics, think of an example today where an attempt to be inclusive seems to have spilt over into a situation that is increasingly self-centred and exclusive. What are the marks of the two communities and where are the tension points?
- How does our understanding of justice and the suffering of the innocent change when read against a backdrop of a family unit or local group, rather than the world? (Genesis 18)
- Distinguish 'judgments after' (when we affirm the voice or action of God with hindsight) from 'judgments before or during', to redefine the meaning of faith and trust.
- Think about two or three recent natural disasters. See if you can find the hand of God in them, or coming out of them.

- How many situations can you think of where 'Isaac' was sacrificed out of loyalty to the old, and what were the consequences? How many can you identify where the old was abandoned for the new, and what were the benefits?

FURTHER READING

Charles M Laymon (ed.), *The Interpreter's One Volume Commentary on the Bible*, Abingdon Press, 1971.

Gerhard von Rad, *Genesis* (Old Testament Library), SCM, 1961.

R.N. Whybray, 'Genesis' in John Barton and John Muddiman (eds.), *The Oxford Bible Commentary*, OUP, 2001.

Narrative readings of the Bible:

David M. Gunn and Danna Nolan Fewell, *Narrative in the Hebrew Bible* (Oxford Bible Series), OUP, 1993.

J.P. Fokkelman, *Reading Biblical Narrative: An Introductory Guide*, Westminster John Knox Press, 1999.

Hagar, life in the wilderness and Hagar's children:

Phyllis Trible, *Texts of Terror*, SCM, 1984.

Trevor Dennis, *The Book of Books*, Lion, 2003.

Gerald O. West, *Reading Other-wise: Socially Engaged Biblical Scholars Reading with their Local Communities*, Society of Biblical Literature, 2007.

Dee Brown, *Bury My Heart at Wounded Knee*, Vintage, 1991.

Jane Harrison's play, *Stolen*, about five Aboriginal people from the 'stolen generations', and a film, *Rabbit-Proof Fence*, in which a 14-year-old Aborigine girl escapes with her sister and cousin from a 1930s Australian government camp intended to forcibly assimilate them into white society.

Luke's strange and sacred journeys

The author of the two-volume work Luke–Acts has a distinctive literary style and several distinctive theological concerns, and is, above all, a consummate storyteller. This week we will be considering one of the distinctive features of his writing—his concern with journeys. For Luke, interesting things happen on journeys: the Christian life is seen as dynamic rather than settled (Christians are described as 'people who 'belong to the Way', Acts 9:2); to travel is as important as to arrive; the direction of travel and the destination are always to be borne in mind; and, of greatest importance, it is on journeys that we encounter God.

The psychologist of religion Kenneth Pargament describes religion as a 'search for significance in ways relating to the sacred' (*The Psychology of Religion and Coping*, p. 32). That is, both the goal of the search and the ways to that goal are sacred. Luke would agree, for he is a writer who is interested in space and time, journeys and destinations, means and ends, but, above all, in our meetings with sacred strangers along the way.

All Bible quotations are from the New Revised Standard Version.

17–23 January

1 The road to Jericho

Luke 10:25–37

A lawyer approaches Jesus and asks about the means to achieve his sacred goal, the inheritance of eternal life. Jesus, himself the fulfilment of the Torah, starts where his questioner feels comfortable—with the Torah. They agree that within it can be found the words of eternal life. Yet the lawyer has an instinct that there may be something more. Perhaps that is why he has come to Jesus in the first place. He wants Jesus to unpack the law for him, to take things further. In response, Jesus takes him, as it were, on a journey.

Jesus asks the lawyer to imagine that he is travelling along a road well known for its dangerous brigands, who prey on travellers. He is mugged, brutally assaulted and left naked and bleeding, completely helpless. As he lies in the road, two religious professionals come along, one after the other. They know that the Torah requires love of neighbour; they are part of a religious system that is aimed at enabling people to come near to their God with confidence. Yet, despite seeing the man, they do not draw near and they show no love of their neighbour. Indeed, by distancing themselves they estrange themselves from the helpless victim; he is no longer their neighbour.

Then a real stranger comes along the road. From the victim's perspective, he is ethnically and religiously distant, and also socially inferior. Yet the stranger sees, is overcome with compassion and draws near. In so doing, he proves the injured man to be his neighbour and, in loving his neighbour, he obeys the Torah. Indeed, in him God comes close to this man. In this, the stranger stands for Jesus, who comes to God's battered and helpless people as their saviour and their great high priest.

The help is delivered by the wrong person—the stranger. He is not a religious professional, he has 'no form or majesty that we should look at him, nothing in his appearance that we should desire him' (Isaiah 53:2), and yet here he is graciously offering salvation. All that the suffering, naked man can do is to accept the costly tender care that is offered to him. And we, so often battered and helpless ourselves, are told to 'go and do likewise', to cease our sacred striving and simply to let the sacred stranger come and find us.

2 The road home

Luke 15:11–24

The stories we know as 'The good Samaritan' and 'The prodigal son' can be understood as a pair, for the situation of the homeward-bound son and the mugging victim are similar in many ways. Both characters are on the road. Both are in desperate places. Both are seen by a man from whom they have been estranged, a man who is overwhelmed with compassion and who, at great cost to himself, goes out of his way to draw near to the one who needs help.

There are, of course, differences. The prodigal son's trouble is much more of his own making than that of the man on the road to Jericho; he has got himself into a desperate place by actively choosing to 'travel to a distant country' (v. 13), and so to separate himself as far as he can from the father who loves him. As he has made his own trouble, he also has to make the decision to get out of trouble. He 'comes to himself' as he remembers what life was like in the place he left behind him (v. 17), starts to aspire to become the person he was really meant to be and, crucially, decides to get up, turn around and journey home.

As he journeys, weak and soiled, while he is still far off from his aspiration, far off from his destination, with his intention to make things right through confession as yet unrealised, a stranger runs down the road towards him and takes him in his arms. With the embrace the estrangement is over: the two men are again father and son. The journey is not done, however. The two complete it together, the son now under the protection of his father, and there is extravagant celebration because a man who had effectively ceased to exist has come to himself and, in so doing, has come home.

Kenneth Pargament says something else about religion: it comes to life in critical situations. It is so often when our backs are against the wall that we turn, and return, to Christ. The turning may be slow and grudging but it is also like an awakening—a coming to ourselves—and, as Christ runs to meet us and support our stumbling steps, we find to our surprise that we too have come home.

3 The road to Jerusalem

Luke 9:51—10:1; 13:33–35

It is Luke, of all the evangelists, who reminds us most strongly that Jesus' ministry was itinerant. Ten out of Luke's 24 chapters are devoted to Jesus' journey from Galilee to Jerusalem. It is a long and winding road, and along the way Jesus heals people like the woman with the curved spine (13:11–17), teaches and tells stories in which journeying features, such as the parable of the great banquet (14:16–24), and is received by people like Zacchaeus (19:2–10) and Martha (10:38). He also sends out 70 disciples on the way as his ambassadors, with instructions to break bread, heal the sick and proclaim the kingdom of God.

Jesus demands that his followers emulate his lifestyle. There is to be no looking back, no attachment to the marks of a settled existence. The love of God is to be shown in abundance to those who will receive it, and those who will not receive it are to be left alone, not persecuted.

Jesus' great journey, with all its marks of the coming kingdom, is important in itself; but it is also a journey with a destination. Luke makes it clear that Jesus is completely focused on Jerusalem, and it is the nature of the destination that renders the journey strange. For, while proclaiming a message of good news, Jesus is travelling with his eyes wide open to meet a fate of rejection and violent death. He longs and yearns for it to be otherwise, but he travels to it all the same.

There are times on the Christian journey when we will be settled, our lives marked by certainties and routines. Our call then is to receive Christ, to welcome him into our dwelling place. For many of us, there will also be times when we are called to get up and follow Christ, to live in transition, to abandon the safety of what is familiar for the risk of the road. This may involve literal travel to strange and dangerous places, or perhaps a change in lifestyle so that we inhabit a risky place; or it may involve a journeying forward in our understanding of God and ourselves. Such a journey may be painful, because in order to be in transition we have to leave behind our settled assumptions about ourselves, about God and about his universe.

4 The road to Emmaus

Luke 24:13–33

The two disciples journeying on the road to Emmaus are in pain, for they are questioning their settled assumptions. Luke tells us that they look 'sad' and that they are 'talking and discussing' (vv. 15, 17). Their journey is a flight from the scene of a deeply traumatic event. The fate that Jesus foresaw for himself has been realised. It made sense to Jesus but it does not make sense to these disciples. They had reached a settled position. A wonderful prophet, 'mighty in word and deed', had come upon the scene (v. 19). He promised much; what he said made sense of life; he offered hope for a happy ending for the people of God. But it had all ended in shameful failure, terrifying violence and, finally, death. Along with the grief for what might have been there is confusion and perplexity. This is the nature of psychological trauma: it breaks into our settled place by shattering our assumptions.

When this happens, our natural response is to shut down, to retreat into ourselves or, like these disciples, to run away. There is increasing evidence that coming to terms with trauma—rebuilding our shattered assumptions so that we can face the world again—is really possible only if we have a wise friend who will get alongside us, enable us to feel safe and show us how our assumptions may still hold good, even in the light of the traumatic events that have assaulted them.

This is precisely what the stranger does with these two disciples. He comes alongside them on the way, walks with them and engages with their perplexity. He starts to connect the recent dark events with their previous settled assumptions about the world—a world in which God is sovereign, just and trustworthy. He shows them that the crucified Messiah is consistent with, not in conflict with, the God they thought they knew. Their hearts burn, because they realise that, indeed, God and his universe are not as they thought, and that this is not a message of despair but of unimaginable possibilities. They are turned around.

When the penny finally drops as the stranger breaks bread at the table, their energised response to this encounter with the risen Christ is immediately to get up and journey again, to turn back to the scene of the action, back to the gathered community of the Church.

5 The road to Damascus

Acts 26:9–18

The disciples on the road to Emmaus were escaping trauma. Saul of Tarsus was trying to avoid it. Jesus of Nazareth and his followers had got under his skin, and they shouldn't have. He had very well settled assumptions about God and his universe: 'as to the law, a Pharisee; as to zeal, a persecutor of the church'. He also had some settled assumptions about himself: 'circumcised on the eighth day, a member of the people of Israel, of the tribe of Benjamin, a Hebrew born of Hebrews… as to righteousness under the law, blameless' (Philippians 3:5–6).

This strange group of people worshipped the crucified one, something that horrified Saul, for, according to Deuteronomy 21:23, 'Anyone hung on a tree is under God's curse' (see Galatians 3:13)—and yet, they got to him. In some strange way their lives and their message challenged his settled assumptions, and when challenge becomes so compelling that it can no longer be ignored, it turns into trauma. So Saul avoids it—indeed, resists it—at all costs. He sets about systematically destroying his source of discomfort with single-minded zeal. We might reflect that there are some very public anti-Christian polemicists who seem to be in a similar pitiable situation today.

While he is journeying on the job, he is stopped in his tracks. That is another characteristic of trauma—it interrupts goal-directed activity—and it seems as if Saul is indeed traumatised. (The blindness and loss of appetite that Luke recounts in Acts 9 may be indicative of this.) Saul falls to the ground and a stranger calls him by name. The stranger asks about Saul's inner motives and remarks that in his quest, Saul is hurting himself. In so doing, the speaker shows deep knowledge—and therefore love—of this human being he has chosen as his own.

What we really require in life, perhaps even more than to be known and loved, is to be genuinely needed. Here Christ offers Saul the best gift of all. He encourages him, like the prodigal son, to come to himself, to be the person he is truly meant to be, to stop pursuing those who belong to the Way and instead to pursue the Way himself. He gives Saul a proper job, to journey throughout the world telling everyone of the strange and inescapable love he encountered on the road.

6 The road to Gaza

Acts 8:26–39

The risen Christ told Paul to get up from the ground (Acts 9:6; 26:16). This instruction to disciples to 'get up' or 'arise' occurs frequently in the New Testament. As I have written elsewhere, 'Being raised with Christ entails a move from passive to active, from relaxed to alert, from weak to strong, from sick to well, from dead to alive, from "the world below" to "the world above" (John 8:23), and—perhaps most of all—from lowly to exalted status' (*Jesus and the Gospel Women*, p. xiii). Saul the Pharisee becomes Paul the apostle to the Gentiles, and in his mind there is no doubt at all that his status has been superlatively raised.

The apostle Philip is also told to get up and take the wilderness road (v. 26), to leave his comfort zone. It's not just the road that is uncomfortable. There is a strange man awaiting him—African, Gentile and a eunuch. Philip seems to require an extra prompt to approach him, to prove himself neighbour to this man (v. 29). The prompt is provided in no uncertain terms by the Holy Spirit, who, like a satnav, imperiously guides him to change course and come alongside the man where he is. Philip readily obeys, having to run to catch the chariot.

The situation of the Ethiopian is rather like that of the disciples on the road to Emmaus: he is perplexed and struggling with the vivid description of shame and violence encountered in a sacred text that he presumably hopes will offer him enlightenment, if not life itself. He is searching for significance in a way related to the sacred. Then a stranger draws near and starts to make sense of it all for him, and his heart burns in response, so that he desires immediately to claim the good news for himself by being baptised.

Philip accompanies the Ethiopian on this next stage of his journey, also. They go down into the depths of the water together, and together arise—get up—to new life. In doing all of this, Philip is becoming more and more like the Lord he follows. He takes a wilderness road, draws near to the stranger, travels with him for a while on the way, and brings him salvation and new life.

Guidelines

There are some recurring themes running through these journeys in Luke's writings. First, they are mostly marked by meetings between strangers. The stranger sometimes comes alongside the traveller, sometimes runs towards the traveller, sometimes blocks the way, sometimes crosses from one side of the road to the other, but always draws near. The journeys always have a clear destination, but the travellers don't always arrive where they expected. The travellers make interesting moves of all sorts, but the general direction is onwards and upwards, for it is through an encounter with Christ and his messengers that people are raised up. The journeys are full of difficulties and dangers, but they are not dull. The meeting with the stranger nudges people into a new way of seeing things, which enables them to accept the love that is offered them with joy.

Second, and perhaps surprisingly, these journeys involve what we might now describe as 'word and sacrament'. The 70 disciples are sent out to eat as well as to heal and proclaim. The stranger on the road to Emmaus begins by expounding the scriptures and ends by breaking bread. The stranger on the road to Gaza begins by expounding the scriptures and ends by baptising a convert. These journeys heal and feed the travellers at several levels.

Finally, the journeys do not depict just the many ways in which we are met by Christ, but also what it means to receive him, to follow him and to walk his way.

You are older than the world can be,
You are younger than the life in me.
Ever old and ever new,
Keep me travelling along with you.
SYDNEY CARTER

FURTHER READING

J. Collicutt McGrath, *Jesus and the Gospel Women*, SPCK, 2009.
J. Duff & J. Collicutt McGrath, *Meeting Jesus: Human Responses to a Yearning God*, SPCK, 2006.
K. Pargament, *The Psychology of Religion and Coping: Theory, Research and Practice*, Guilford, 1997.

Apologetics

What do you think of when you hear the word 'Apologetics'? It sounds a bit like apologising, as if Christians should say sorry for believing in Christ. For some, the word may conjure up ideas of dusty books and dry intellectualising about the Christian faith. For others, apologetics has meant totally irrelevant arguments about minute details of the Bible or Christian theology. Neither of these descriptions cut it. The word 'apologetics' comes from the Greek word *apologia*, which literally means a reasoned defence. We are reminded of the lawyer in a court room who speaks on behalf of the accused, articulately defending the individual from the attack of the prosecutor and asking questions of the witnesses so as to bring out the truth of the matter.

Put simply, apologetics is the ability to talk to non-Christian friends, colleagues and family members about Christ in a convincing and meaningful way, so that they come to a point of decision for themselves. It is the task of every Christian, like a lawyer in a court room, to be able to respond to the questions of non-believers coherently and persuasively. 1 Peter 3:15–16 puts it like this: 'But in your hearts set apart Christ as Lord. Always be prepared to give an answer to everyone who asks you to give the reason for the hope that you have. But do this with gentleness and respect, keeping a clear conscience.'

Apologetics is very much on the agenda for many of us again today as we find ourselves on the receiving end of questions about our faith in Christ. The rise of rampant secularism, articulate atheism and the multi-faith agenda, as well as other challenges facing us as Christians in Europe, have all contributed to these questions. In this fortnight of Bible reading notes, we will be exploring the whole area of apologetics, looking in particular at the questions of identity and suffering in the first week and at the relevance and reliability of the Bible in the second week.

Quotations are taken from the New International Version of the Bible.

1 A reason for the hope

1 Peter 3:15–16

We know from the beginning of the letter of 1 Peter that it was written to 'God's elect, strangers in the world, scattered…' (1:1), and so the command to 'give an answer' is not addressed to a group of specialists or even to a geographical group in a particular cultural situation: it is given to the whole Church. In other words, apologetics is not a specialist activity intended only for intellectuals who enjoy arguing about ideas, nor is it commended only to those who consider themselves to be 'evangelists': it is for all of us.

We can also see from this passage that the context for apologetics is holiness: our Christian attitudes and actions in the world are vital. Peter assumes that we live a vibrant, dynamic, Christ-filled life and that, as a consequence, people will ask us 'why' questions. All of this means that we need to 'be prepared'. The Greek word used here is *gymnasio*, which carries the connotation of physical fitness. Getting fit involves exercise and effort. In the same way, being prepared for conversations about the Lord will require preparation and a kind of apologetic fitness that takes some effort on our part.

Peter talks of giving an answer for the 'reason for the hope'. There is a *logion*—a 'reason'—for what we believe. People believe all kinds of things about reality, whether they be superstitions, old wives' tales, conspiracy theories or the official line. But Peter reminds us that the gospel makes sense. There are good reasons to believe that God exists, that he made the world, that Christ was God in human form and that he died for us. The message of the gospel, Christ crucified and resurrected, is capable of being explained and understood.

Finally we are encouraged to consider our mode of communication: we are to do our apologetics 'with gentleness and respect'. So much of our witness hangs on our attitude; it is easily possible to win arguments and lose people. When we speak about Christ, let there be evidence of his existence in our own lives, let us give thoughtful answers that demonstrate some preparation and stand up to scrutiny, and let us point to the reason for our hope—Christ and his gospel.

2 Why are Christians hypocrites?

1 John 1:8—2:6

When asked to say what was the most difficult question posed to him about the Christian faith, a Christian leader responded: 'If Christ transforms us, why do we see so little evidence of this in some of his followers?' This is not to say that there aren't many wonderful individual Christians and communities of Christians, rather that a widespread objection to the Christian faith is the quality of life displayed by many Christians. Bertrand Russell's daughter, Katharine Tait, wrote, 'I would have liked to convince my father that I had found what he had been looking for, the ineffable something he had longed for all his life... But it was hopeless. He had known too many blind Christians, bleak moralists who sucked the joy from life and persecuted their opponents; he would never have been able to see the truth they were hiding' (*My Father Bertrand Russell*, Harcourt Brace Jovanovich, 1975, p. 189).

'Christians are hypocrites' is a phrase that we often hear when involved in apologetics. The word 'hypocrite' can mean 'a person who acts in contradiction to his or her stated beliefs or feelings'. The question here is one of authenticity. 1 John 1:8–9 anticipates that, as Christians, we will fail and that we need to ask for forgiveness when this happens. We may not be the best examples of Christianity, but we pray that this will not stop others from seeing Christ for themselves.

However, if becoming a Christian has made no difference at all to an individual, then we must question the genuineness of that individual's faith. The Bible certainly does this: 1 John 2:4 is a real challenge to us. Jesus was very harsh about people who claimed to be religious but whose hearts and lives didn't match up to their outward projections, and he taught that not everyone who claimed to be his follower actually was one (Matthew 7:21). This is a clear call for authenticity. In the face of the question of hypocrisy, one of the greatest apologetics is a life lived for Christ and not for self. It is also a life lived in humility, demonstrating our human need for forgiveness and reminding the world that the Christian faith is not for the morally superior but for those who recognise their need for a saviour.

3 Good and evil?

Genesis 1:26–31

This passage talks of a good God creating a good world and specifically making human beings as creatures in his image. In 1 John 4:8 we read that 'God is love', and so creatures created in God's image are able to love. If the humans whom God made were forced to love him and each other, they would not be human at all. They would be machines, and love would not truly exist. As C.S. Lewis writes, 'Free will, though it makes evil possible, is also the only thing that makes possible any love or goodness or joy worth having. A world of automata—of creatures that worked like machines— would hardly be worth creating' (*Mere Christianity*, 1964, p. 49).

For love to exist, it must be freely given. But then, where does evil come from? Isn't it also a created entity, as Muslims claim? No. In the Bible, evil is a counterfeit of good: it is not part of creation. As Genesis 1:31 reminds us, 'God saw all that he made, and it was very good.' C.S. Lewis calls evil 'a parasite, not an original thing' (*Mere Christianity*, p. 50). The devil was not created as evil: he is Lucifer, a good angel who is fallen. An illustration may help us here. In order to make a room dark, we do not switch darkness on; we switch the light off. Darkness is a negative entity that can be explained only as the absence of light. So it is with evil. It is a subversion of good rather than a created entity itself. Because true holiness is love, it can operate only in an atmosphere of freedom. Thus morality as a function of freedom in finite creatures has to reckon with the possibility that good may fall and produce evil.

An infinitely moral, holy God placed his creation under the stewardship of human beings who were created by him to share his moral characteristics. It is because we have rebelled against God that we have let loose fractures in relationships—with ourselves, with others, with God and with nature. Evil is good that has fallen.

4 When disasters come

Luke 13:1–5

In this remarkable passage (which we shall study again tomorrow), Jesus is faced with a question that we often ask ourselves as Christians: 'Did such and such a disaster happen because of the sin of the people involved?' Jesus is unequivocally clear in his answer: he draws no direct link between the disaster and the sins of the individuals who suffer. But he does seem to remind us that such disasters can function as a reminder to all of us that one day we ourselves will face judgment.

Often, though, disasters cause people to question the very existence of God. Whether it be an evil act of abuse, such as Pilate's mixing the blood of his victims with sacrifices (v. 1), or the seemingly random suffering of somebody who dies in an earthquake under a collapsed building (v. 4), couldn't God have intervened? Shouldn't God have stopped these things from happening? From the atheist perspective, the 'survival of the fittest' and the equivalence of human and animal life mean that, as Richard Dawkins has written, 'If the universe were just electrons and selfish genes, meaningless tragedies... are exactly what we should expect, along with equally meaningless good fortune' (*River out of Eden*, Harper-Collins, 1995, pp. 132–133). It is only if human life is sacred, God-given and thus intrinsically precious that these questions of suffering have any purchase.

The question of suffering leads Christians inexorably to face our own human condition and need for a saviour. The fact that plate tectonic movement is necessary for the earth to be life-permitting is cold comfort for people directly affected by earthquakes, but is it really fair to blame God for the death of those who live in such regions when, as a human race, we have the technology to build in such a way as to withstand earthquakes and preserve life? Is it a coincidence that it is the world's poorest who are so often the victims of apparently 'random' disasters? Is it not, again, the reality of human selfishness and sin that causes the pain and suffering of so many people?

The question, then, as Jesus refocuses it for us, is: will we repent? Will we examine our own hearts and ask the question, in the face of others' suffering, are we ourselves ready to face judgment? After all, the God who judges is the one who makes life sacred and who values every human life as infinitely precious.

5 Did I deserve it?

Luke 13:1–5

Looking at this passage again, we ask the question that Jesus was asked: what about people who suffer at the hands of an evil abuser? Pilate mixed the blood of these Galileans with his sacrifice. They suffered horrendously. Why? Did they in some way deserve what happened to them? In this case, Jesus answers, 'No.'

But why ask the question? Suffering is complex for the Christian, since it can be a direct consequence of sin, whether that be sinful abuse by another person or our own fault. It may be that we suffer the consequences of our own folly, contracting cancer after smoking for years, or ending up alone after destroying our own marriage by having an affair. Sometimes it is possible to see the reason for our suffering in our own actions. More frequently, we suffer at the hands of others. Living as I do in a deprived community of London, we encounter the horrific reality of this on a regular basis, in domestic violence, rape, child abuse, contract killings, extortion and theft.

This is the situation with Pilate and the Galileans. From a biblical perspective, such suffering is put into an explanatory context by the beginning and end of the Bible. We see that a world in which love is possible entails human freedom. This choice is abused and, while love is still possible, suffering also becomes part of the picture. However, the God who created the world will also judge the world, and those who appear to get off scot-free in this life, abusing and violating others, will face the judgment of God, as we all will. He will ensure that justice is done in the end.

Again we note that Jesus encourages his hearers to repent. In the face of suffering, whether at the hands of an abuser or through a seemingly random disaster, we are challenged by the reality of the human heart, our need for forgiveness and salvation. The Bible engages with suffering as a reality, dealing with human moral responsibility but also introducing us to a God who enters into the suffering world and suffers himself on the cross, in Christ, to redeem humanity.

6 Why do bad things happen to good people?

Job 4:1–9; 27:1–6; 42:7–9

Why do bad things happen to good people and good things happen to bad people? Is there a causal link between sin and suffering? When suffering comes, can we make a direct link between a victim and their own moral failings? I return to these questions again because I am so frequently surprised to see how much purchase the idea has among Christians.

We must be careful not to answer these apologetic questions about the causes of suffering too hastily. As we have seen, our own sin and folly can bring trouble down upon our own heads, just as human selfishness and greed can harm other people. Suffering is often the result of sin—whether our own or somebody else's—but we can be sure of one thing, and that is that there is no rule of karma within the Christian worldview.

The pervasive influence of this Hindu doctrine upon the Western world appears to have infiltrated the Church. Karma is a law of cause and effect: 'what goes around comes around'. The cycle of karma, in Hinduism, continually turns through multiple incarnations, with cause and effect following on from one another in repeated life cycles. Such an idea is the ultimate denial of grace, as well as severely underestimating the complexity of suffering in the world. The Bible does not allow us to draw a simple, clear connection between individual sin and suffering.

The book of Job in the Old Testament tells the story of a man who loses everything—his family, his wealth and his health. He has always been a righteous man but his friends assume that he must have sinned to deserve this state of affairs. Job insists on his innocence and, in the end, is vindicated by God. The story of Job will not allow Christians to fall into the idea that karma rules—and nor will the New Testament, since the apostles and many other wonderful Christians suffered and died gruesomely.

Sometimes we will suffer and there will be no direct reason for it other than our humanness and the fact that we live in a real, fallen world. The psalmists and prophets continually ask why the righteous suffer and the wicked prosper (see, for example, Psalm 73:3–13; Jeremiah 12:1), and at least a part of the biblical answer is that this is a consequence of living in a fallen world as described for us in Genesis 3. There are other reasons why Christians suffer, the most obvious of which is that we may be suffering for our faith. Persecution has been a constant companion for followers of Jesus from the very earliest moments of the Church to the present day. Suffering comes for lots of different reasons, but karma isn't one of them.

Guidelines

This week we have looked at some of the apologetic questions around the issue of suffering. We have remembered that God made a good world within which humans have the capacity to love and to make choices. We have seen that evil is a parasite—it is not an original thing but an absence of love and goodness—and that it is the consequence of our choices as humans. We have asked some of the questions that the psalmists ask about the suffering of good people, and considered the example of Job. We have thought about the victims of abusers and 'random' disasters and we have considered the reality of God's judgment as a biblical context within which to think about suffering.

The next obvious question, then, is why God does not always intervene on behalf of his followers in order to prevent or alleviate their suffering. It is possible for suffering to have a positive role in the life of the believer, purifying motives and attitudes, but there is also a theological context which may help us to understand suffering from a biblical perspective, especially as God does sometimes intervene miraculously, delivering people from danger, disease or death. This can be called the 'now and not yet' of the kingdom of God. Jesus' coming to earth and leaving his followers with the Holy Spirit inaugurated his kingdom, and so we read, 'The kingdom of God is within you' (Luke 17:21). This means that 'the blind receive sight... and the good news is preached to the poor'(Luke 7:22). But the kingdom is also still to come: there is a future hope (Matthew 6:10). When Jesus returns, there will be a final judgment and a new heaven and earth. This is when suffering will finally end. Miraculous interventions in the present are signs pointing towards this future reality. They are not deserved badges of God's special favour for the individual who is healed or helped, but visible signs for everyone to see that the future judgment and bliss are really coming.

When we have the opportunity to 'give a reason for the hope that we have', apologetics can help us to answer the questions that people ask, as well as to engage with the questions we ask ourselves.

1 Are the Gospels myths invented by humans?

2 Peter 1:16–21

In this passage, Peter tells us that the gospel is history: these are not 'cleverly invented stories', myths with a good moral meaning, but true. He himself was an eyewitness to the events of Jesus' life and he references the baptism of Jesus and his transfiguration as key events at which he was present (Mark 1:9–11; 9:2–8).

Mark's Gospel was based on Peter's testimony, and here we are encouraged to take it seriously as truthful and historical. Respected scholarship on the manuscripts of the Gospels points to early composition of the texts, leaving no time for mythology or hagiography to develop in the period between the events and the writing of the accounts: 'The interval, then, between the dates of original composition and the earliest extant evidence becomes so small as to be in fact negligible, and the last foundation for any doubt that the Scriptures have come down to us substantially as they were written has now been removed. Both the authenticity and the general integrity of the books of the New Testament may be regarded as finally established' (Sir Frederic G. Kenyon, *Handbook to the Textual Criticism of the New Testament*, 1901, p. 4).

As Peter tells us, these are not cleverly invented stories. The manuscript evidence for the New Testament is a witness to the Gospels' reliability and authenticity, but the writings of the Church Fathers also testify to these qualities. The Epistle of Clement to the Corinthians (dated AD95) cites verses from the Gospels, Acts, Romans, 1 Corinthians, Ephesians, Titus, Hebrews and 1 Peter. In fact, there are 86,000 New Testament quotations in the writings of the Church Fathers. This means that if the ancient manuscripts already mentioned were to disappear overnight, it would still be possible to reconstruct the entire New Testament with quotations from the Church Fathers, with the exception of 15–20 verses.

Peter tells us that the Bible is not a cleverly invented hoax and that biblical prophecy, in particular, is not fabricated (vv. 20–21): prophets spoke with genuine and truthful motivation, inspired by the Holy Spirit. What a contrast to the sceptics' view of the Bible, but how important for us to know that Peter understood such allegations of fraud and was able to refute them confidently. We should do the same.

2 Can we know what the Bible really means?

John 1:1–14

Do words and texts have any inherent meaning at all? When I read the Bible, does it all just come down to a matter of opinion? Are all interpretations equally valid? Can these texts actually speak to me or do I make them mean what I want?

The issue of whether or not words have any meaning is incredibly important as we look at the Christian faith and as we offer people the source materials about the life of Jesus. If the Bible only means what we make it mean, there is no point reading it in order to discover anything about God.

The idea that there is no ultimate meaning in any text has become extremely powerful in a postmodern context, and it has enormous implications for any communication about the gospel. The philosopher Friedrich Nietzsche commented, 'We cannot get rid of God until we get rid of grammar' (*Twilight of the Idols*, trans. R.J. Hollingdale, Penguin, 1972).

The thinker Jacques Derrida denies that language has any fixed meaning connected to a fixed reality or that it unveils definitive truth. He bemoans the belief that language can have meaning as it causes people to search for some ultimate Word/presence/essence/truth/reality which can serve as the foundation of thought, language and experience—'the transcendental signified' (*Of Grammatology*, trans. G.C. Spivak, Johns Hopkins University Press, 1998, p. 49). He argues that such a God does not actually exist. But doesn't this show us that, unless God exists, language cannot carry meaning? If we want to reject God, we have to undermine language.

In chapter 1 of his Gospel, John asserts that there is a Word—a reference point for reality and meaning—and he tells us that this very Word became flesh and dwelt among us in the person of Christ. If we believe in Jesus, we uphold the possibility that language communicates truth and meaning, and we worship the God in whom all knowledge, meaning and truth originate. Without him as the reference point, so much of the intellectual framework of life, language and existence collapses. As John reminds us, 'In him was life, and that life was the light of men' (v. 4).

3 Why write a Gospel?

Luke 1:1–4; John 20:30–31

When reading the Gospels it is vital to remember that we are handling well-preserved historical documents. These writings provide us with unprecedented access to ancient history and, as such, are worthy of the interest they inspire among Christian believers and non-believers alike. From an apologetics point of view, one of the great strengths of the New Testament is that it does not just give us one perspective on Jesus: we have four accounts that come from different writers and carry slightly different perspectives.

In today's readings, we are given an insight into the expressed intentions of two of the Gospel writers: they are telling us, their readers, why they are writing. This is important because, if we are to assess the veracity and validity of what the Gospels record, we need to come to some conclusions about the motivation of the authors. Luke wrote his gospel as a Gentile believer in Jesus. He was a doctor, a scientific man who did not have the privilege of being one of the twelve disciples who lived with Jesus for three years and knew him incredibly well. Luke expresses his intentions for his Gospel at the beginning of his account. He tells us that although he did not personally witness the events he describes, he has conducted fastidious research with the eyewitnesses and has written a Gospel intended to be 'an orderly account' (v. 3) for other Gentiles, such as Theophilus.

John, on the other hand, was one of the twelve disciples; a Jewish man with profound and personal insights into the life and ministry of Jesus, having lived with him for three years and watched his ministry unfold. John is known as 'the beloved disciple' as it seems that he was exceptionally close to Jesus. He expresses his intentions in writing his Gospel towards the end of his book: he writes so that we, the readers, may also experience life in the name of Jesus.

Both writers have the ring of truth, and it is difficult for the sceptic to impute motives of deception or power-play in the face of this testimony.

The time interval between the events themselves and their written record in the Gospels was too short to have allowed memories to be erased of what had or had not actually happened.

4 The resurrection: evidence for God?

Matthew 28:5–15

There are three established historical facts that are best explained by the resurrection of Jesus. These are not controversial, but are widely accepted by scholars: the fact that Jesus' tomb was found empty, the fact that Jesus appeared to people alive after his death, and the fact that the Christian faith began at all.

Firstly, the evidence indicates that Jesus' tomb was found empty by a group of his female followers on Sunday morning. Women were not considered reliable witnesses in a court of law in that culture, so, if the early believers had wanted to make a false story seem true, why would women have been cited as some of the key witnesses? No other burial tradition exists; whether by friend or foe, the tomb was acknowledged as empty.

Secondly, the evidence indicates that, on separate occasions, different individuals and groups saw physical appearances of Jesus alive after his death. Christ appeared to 500 people all at once; he appeared to a sceptic (Thomas), an unbeliever (James the brother of Jesus), and an enemy (Saul) (see John 20:26–28; 1 Corinthians 15:6–8).

Thirdly, Christianity began in the middle of the first century, but why? After all, Jesus was crucified by the Romans, and a dead Messiah does not provide much of a rallying point. The disciples claimed that God had raised Jesus from the dead, and they proclaimed this message everywhere they went. They held to this belief despite the fact that Jewish culture had no concept of individual resurrection: a corporate resurrection at the end of time was what was expected.

These elements and many others come together to form a powerful case for the bodily resurrection of Christ from the grave. The resurrection appears to be by far the best explanation for the historical realities. Apologetics reminds us of these evidences, encouraging us in our own walk with Christ and equipping us to speak for him in our daily lives.

5 Miracles... seriously?

John 6:16–21

When we are doing apologetics and answering questions about the Bible, following on from conversations about the manuscript tradition of the New Testament, we can expect to hear further comments, such as 'Just because the manuscripts are reliable, that doesn't make their content true.' Indeed, it is true that no one argues for the historicity of Homer's mythology. The manuscripts of his writings may be reasonably intact but that does not make his subject matter reliable or accurate historical material. Aren't the Gospels on the same kind of level? Aren't they just mythological stories with true moral value but very little historical reality? Surely, accounts involving people walking on water and water turning into wine weren't meant to be taken as historically true?

A powerful reason for people to reject the content of the Gospels and the rest of the Bible as true is its recording of miraculous events. The root of this rejection is often an assumed framework in which miracles are a logical impossibility. Such scepticism is based on the ideas of the philosopher David Hume (1711–76), who argued that all objects of human inquiry are either 'relations of ideas' (mathematical statements and definitions) or 'matters of fact'—everything which can be known and tested empirically. But there is a major problem with this: as one philosopher comments, 'The statement that "only analytic or empirical propositions are meaningful" is not itself an analytic (true by definition) or empirical statement. Hence, by its own criteria it is meaningless' (*Baker Encyclopedia of Christian Apologetics*, Baker Academic, 1998, p. 341).

In other words, a sceptic's reasons for rejecting the gospel would negate his or her own worldview. This kind of a priori commitment to the falseness of the Gospels or the non-possibility of any miraculous occurrence is a form of closed-mindedness. The basis on which these views are held, philosophical materialism, is not itself logically consistent and deserves to be challenged.

As we read this account of a miracle in scripture, we see that the disciples observing Jesus were 'terrified' (v. 19). Christ challenges the expectations and worldviews of those he encounters, and his miracles are intended to have this effect. The question is: are we open-minded enough to consider the challenge with which he presents us?

6 Isn't Christianity sexist?

Luke 8:1–3

Many people have the idea that the Bible is somehow sexist, out of date and antiquated in its approach to gender. For some, this is a significant hindrance to serious consideration of the claims of Christ. Perhaps they have become disillusioned by divisions in the Church or simply feel that the Church has kept women and other minorities down. When we look at the example of Jesus, however, nothing could be further from the truth. In a culture where the idea of a woman travelling around with a group of men, or having the status of disciple to a rabbi, was seriously questionable, Jesus had a number of women included in his travelling circle. By mentioning these women by name, Luke's Gospel offers them praise and gratitude for their financial contributions to the ministry of Jesus.

A sharp contrast may be seen here with authors such as Ben Sirach of Jerusalem (c.195BC), who reflect the more prevalent attitude of the culture, with statements such as 'Bad temper, insolence and shame hold sway where the wife supports the husband' (Sirach 25:22). Jesus travels with women in his group of disciples and allows them to contribute financially to the needs of the group.

When we read the Gospels, we will also discover that women played an important and prominent role as historic witnesses to the central events surrounding Jesus Christ. It was a group of women who stood at the foot of the cross, watching Jesus die and hearing his last words (John 19:25), and it was a group of women who first witnessed the resurrection of Christ (Luke 24:1–10). Again, it is striking for us to remember that the word of women was perceived as having less value than that of men in their culture. It is therefore enormously important that the most significant events of Jesus' death and resurrection were witnessed first-hand by women.

Apologetics can help us with this kind of question. When faced with the charge of sexism, the Bible itself tells an entirely different story: man and woman were created equal in the sight of God (Genesis 1:27) and women are encouraged, taught and honoured in the Gospel narratives.

Guidelines

Apologetics has many functions in the life of the Christian: it helps us to share our faith and deal with the spiritual and sceptical questions of our non-believing friends, but it is also spiritually significant for us personally as we go deeper in our own walk with God. Nothing less than a genuine, personal and fulfilling relationship with the person of Christ will equip us in such a way that we are not ourselves distracted or deceived by fine-sounding arguments, which try to drag us away from God. There may well be many sophisticated questions and arguments to be heard, but we are not to be deceived by them (Colossians 2:4). We can be protected from such deception by being completely rooted in God's word and filled by Christ. In Colossians 2:8, Paul warns his readers—not sceptical unbelievers but true Christians—not to be taken captive in their minds. There is a spiritual battle for the mind, and we too need to watch that we are not taken captive by wrong ideas about God and his world.

So, as we reflect at the end of two weeks of thinking about apologetics, whether it be historical, evidential and textual apologetics or questions about suffering or human experience, we remember that our foundation is the person of Christ and his word—a foundation that does stand up to scrutiny. We remember that our own questions and the questions of our friends are not to be feared; rather, they present opportunities to explore the 'reason for the hope we have'.

FURTHER READING

Paul Copan, *True for You but Not for Me: Countering the Slogans that Leave Christians Speechless*, Bethany House, 2009.

Norman Geisler, *When Skeptics Ask: A Handbook on Christian Evidences*, Baker Books, 2008.

Josh McDowell, *Evidence that Demands a Verdict*, Authentic, 1999.

Alister McGrath, *Bridge Building: Effective Christian Apologetics*, IVP, 1994.

Lee Strobel, *The Case for Christ: A Journalist's Personal Investigation of the Evidence for Jesus*, Zondervan, 1998.

Ravi Zacharias, *Can Man Live Without God?*, W Publishing, 2004.

Matthew 15—20

We begin this year's study of Matthew's Gospel around the halfway point, before Jesus sets out from Galilee in the north for his final climactic visit to Jerusalem.

In these six chapters, it seems that Jesus is bombarded with questions from all sides—from his disciples, his opponents, and others who seek healing, deliverance or spiritual direction. The questions are urgent and probing, often born of a desire to 'place' him in a particular category, to allow his questioners to make a judgment about his identity and his authority.

To some of these enquiries, he chooses not to respond directly. When he does give an answer, it is never predictable. Rather than allowing others to categorise him within their limited worldview, he continually attempts to broaden their horizons. His kingdom and his rule as Messiah within that kingdom will not be as they expect: the generosity and grace of God extend far beyond the boundaries of Israel, and his followers are challenged with higher standards of holiness and humility than they would have imagined.

Ultimately, the questioners find themselves asked to examine their own hearts, to decide whether they are prepared to abandon their personal agendas and follow him.

7–13 February

1 Obedience to God's word

Matthew 15:1–12

We join the story of Jesus, as told by Matthew, in that phase of his Galilean ministry when he was beginning to encounter an increasing amount of opposition. His teaching and healing have caused quite a stir; now even some of the religious hierarchy from Jerusalem have decided it is time come up north to investigate (v. 1).

The Pharisees had the noble desire that God should act to redeem his people in line with Old Testament prophecy. Yet they were convinced that this would happen only when the 'people of the land' were observing the

Jewish law and doing so in accordance with the 'traditions of the elders': hence their concern when they discovered that Jesus had been modelling to his disciples a rather lax approach to hand-washing. Surely, they would have argued, such rituals needed to be observed strictly—not least in a frontier region like Galilee, where the Jewish people were constantly living side by side with pagan Gentiles. Such 'boundary markers', which help-fully distinguished God's true people from their neighbours, were critically important. Yet here was Jesus, dangerously compromising them.

Jesus will give a reply on this precise issue (see tomorrow's reading) but first he homes in on a deeper, underlying problem: the way the Pharisees use their commitment to 'tradition' as a means of sidestepping the explicit demands of God's word. (The example he cites consisted of people being persuaded to give any surplus income into the temple's treasury, rather than being allowed to use it for the upkeep of their parents.) Jesus clearly had a high view of scripture, seeing the Ten Commandments as coming directly from God (v. 4) and seeing Isaiah's prophetic words as applicable to people in his own day (vv. 8–9; Isaiah 29:13). He gave an evident prior-ity to the 'word of God' (see also Matthew 4:4).

His followers need to do the same, developing a reverent attitude to-wards God's word and being aware when we are starting to play subtle games with it, in the hope we might be able to escape its clear commands. True worship of God, Jesus teaches, thus involves having our hearts close to God—and this is tested supremely by our openness to God's words and obedience to his commands. Worship without such obedience is 'in vain' (v. 9). Religious traditions in themselves may be quite neutral; the impor-tant question is whether individuals are using them to help them engage with God's word or, rather, as a subtle means of avoiding it.

2 'Unclean' in God's sight

Matthew 15:12–20

The sight of someone retching or vomiting is embarrassing and ugly. So Jesus' saying ('what comes out of a person's mouth makes them unclean'), if taken literally, evokes some unpleasant images. No wonder Peter asks for an explanation of this 'parable' (v. 15) or strange dictum. What on earth is Jesus saying?

Jesus' responses in this 'debriefing' with his disciples reveal some of his masterly teaching skills. First he comments on the personalities of those involved (the Pharisees: vv. 12–14), then on the debate itself (vv. 15–20). The Pharisees think of themselves as reliable guides for the blind (see Romans 2:19), but Jesus says they themselves are 'blind' (Matthew 23:16). He even implies that they are not truly part of God's people (a 'plant' being a biblical picture for Israel: Isaiah 60:21). Chiefly they are blind because they cannot see in Jesus the true fulfilment of their hopes.

Those who follow the Pharisees, Jesus warns, will stumble 'into a pit' (v. 14). 'That won't happen,' Jesus is implying, 'if you follow me.' Jesus here shows no inclination to compromise and no qualms about causing the Pharisees some 'offence' (v. 12). A true teacher or leader recognises those times when clarity of principle takes precedence over mere charity—keeping everybody happy in the short term, but with ruinous consequences for the long term.

Returning to the main debate, Jesus comments in an earthy way about the body's digestive system, but that only shows that his words must not be taken literally. He was talking not about the physical stomach but the spiritual 'heart'—that which signifies a person's deepest realities, what 'makes them tick'. And here Jesus, as a master surgeon, detects ugly weeds in all of us: not just evil words and deeds ('murder', 'adultery', 'slander'/'blasphemies', which flout the Ten Commandments) but 'evil thoughts'. As in the Sermon on the Mount (Matthew 5—7) Jesus locates sin deep down, in our thought life.

This is a chilling indictment of us all, unmasking the reality that we would prefer to hide. Jesus here pithily endorses what is taught so frequently elsewhere in scripture concerning human sin and depravity, and his words leave a profound question unanswered: if we are so radically 'unclean' in God's sight, how can we be washed clean? This then gives extra force to Matthew's portrayal both of Jesus' death (for the 'forgiveness of sins': 26:28) and of his whole life, for his very name, 'Jesus', means 'he will save people from their sins' (1:21). Jesus turns out to be the unique answer to the problem he has uncovered.

3 Grace for the Gentiles

Matthew 15:21–28

In Matthew's next two episodes, Jesus is in Gentile territory. Perhaps needing some quiet space after recent controversies with Israel's leaders, Jesus goes north (into the region of modern Lebanon) and then back round to the south-east of Lake Galilee. Matthew thus has a rare opportunity to show Jesus' dealing directly with Gentiles (see also 8:5–13). How did Jesus approach them?

Initially the answer is surprising. Given that, in our days, we seek racial equality, we might hope that Jesus would treat them exactly the same—and eventually he does, but not without first making a crucial point. Hence his initial refusal to respond to the pleas of the Canaanite woman: 'I was sent only to the lost sheep of Israel' (v. 24; see 10:5–6). It sounds as if Jesus will send her away empty-handed (which is what the disciples themselves are selfishly suggesting: v. 23) because his primary task is to preach the kingdom to his own nation. Worse still, he uses the contemporary Jewish way of referring to all Gentiles as mere 'dogs'—telling her it would be wrong for such 'dogs' to get priority at table over the 'children' (v. 26). After all, it would indeed be horrendous if parents fattened their pets while starving their own offspring!

'But even the dogs,' the woman pluckily retorts, 'eat the crumbs that fall from their master's table!' Effectively she agrees that the Israelites are God's chosen 'children'. She is humbling herself—in comparison to them and to their God whom she recognises as her 'master'. Moreover, she recognises that Jesus acts directly on behalf of Israel's God—he himself being cast in the role of the 'master'—and her talking of 'crumbs' reveals her conviction of how much healing is available, for even a 0.5 per cent share would be sufficient.

Do we have the same humble mindset? If we are Gentile readers of Matthew's Gospel, do we recognise this deep pattern in God's plans—to bring healing to the world by calling Abraham (Genesis 12)? Do we acknowledge that the gospel is 'for the Jews first' and only then for us Gentiles (Romans 2:10) and that we are 'unnatural branches' who have been brought into the olive tree of God's people only by grace (Romans 11)? Gentile arrogance is to be dismissed. So we need to 'know our place' in God's overall purposes; yet, if we emulate the woman's faith in Jesus as the 'master', we discover that it is a place of grace.

4 Feeding the 4000

Matthew 15:29–39

Jesus' foray into Gentile territory continues. Some time later he is found in the hilly area to the south-east of Lake Galilee (what Mark 7:31 rightly calls the 'Decapolis', an area ruled by a federation of ten Greek cities). Jesus had been in this general region before (in the episode of the Gadarene swine: Matthew 8:28–34), but now his arrival causes a large crowd to follow him. They have been with him in this remote area for 'three days' (v. 32), drawn by the evident power of Jesus to heal. They are 'amazed' and 'praise the God of Israel' (v. 31).

That phrase in Matthew provides the key to this passage: as with the Canaanite woman, this is a story about Gentiles outside Israel getting a glimpse of what God is doing within Israel through Jesus. And it neatly explains why Matthew includes this (otherwise seemingly repetitive) story about Jesus multiplying loaves and fishes (see the feeding of the 5000 just above, in 14:13–21): what Jesus has done among the Jewish population, he is now repeating for a Gentile crowd. Some scholars also see a Jew/Gentile parallelism in the numbers: '5000' might reflect the Jewish love of the number five (for example, the five books of Moses); '4000' might reflect the Gentile nations spread out to the four compass points of the earth. In any event, Jesus, even if primarily focused on Israel, is intending to treat both groups equally. So there is more than a hint here that, in due course, what God is doing through Jesus will cause God's blessing to go out to 'all nations' (see 28:19).

So this dramatic feeding miracle will teach us many of the same things that we learn from the feeding of the 5000: Jesus' unique power over the natural world; his expressed 'compassion' (v. 32) for the crowd; his desire to use this episode to teach his disciples and stretch their faith (see 16:9–10). All of these lessons, we can ponder today. In what ways is the risen

Jesus going to stretch our faith in him today? Who are those today who would be the object of his 'compassion'? Yet one of the main points may be to do with God's overflowing generosity. Just above, a Gentile woman would have been content with a few 'crumbs' (v. 27); now there are seven baskets of breadcrumbs left over (v. 37)! Truly the God of Jesus wants to bless people in ways that are extravagant.

5 A wicked generation

Matthew 16:1–12

'Generation Y'; the 'me generation': these labels seek to describe groups in today's society. Here Jesus labels his generation, and he's blunt: it is 'wicked and adulterous' (v. 4; 12:39).

Jesus has returned from Gentile territory and is confronted again by a delegation of Pharisees (joining forces now with their rival Sadducees, Jerusalem's aristocratic ruling party). Again they are checking up on him and ask for a 'sign'—something to report back to their superiors. Of course, Jesus has done numerous miraculous signs; he also gladly sent a report of these signs back to John the Baptist (11:4–5). This time, however, he refuses. After all, the Pharisees have already labelled his exorcisms as demonic (12:24) and will presumably use any 'sign' as evidence against him—perhaps accusing him of leading Israel astray by 'signs and wonders' (Deuteronomy 13:1–5).

So Jesus changes the focus. If they were looking (at best) for a sign of his authority, they should instead be noting the 'signs of the times' (v. 3)—things happening through his ministry that are clear signs of God's imminent judgment. If they can predict that the day's weather will be stormy, why can they not see the storm clouds gathering on their national horizon? Yes, they will be given a sign (the 'sign of Jonah': already explained in 12:39–40 as a reference to Jesus' resurrection), but it will serve as God's warning to this generation (note how Jerusalem would be destroyed exactly 40 years, or one 'generation', later, in AD70).

So the delegation returns to Jerusalem unsatisfied and the battle lines are now drawn more tightly. (When Jesus himself reaches Jerusalem, we can expect the sparks to fly: see chs. 21—23.) For now, Jesus simply warns his disciples (using the imagery of 'yeast', which, in Jewish Passover practice, contaminated the purity of the unleavened bread) not to be led astray by their negative influence.

This incident leaves us today with some important questions: if it is not wrong to ask for the risen Jesus to work in ways that reveal his glory, nevertheless are we asking with a perspective of open faith or, instead, are we being subtly challenging and demanding? As we go through life, do we heed the 'warning signs' or are we the kind of people who have to hit a brick wall before we pick up the signals that we are on the wrong path? And, yes, how would Jesus describe our generation?

6 The Messiah and his Church

Matthew 16:13–20

Throughout Matthew's central chapters, one question has become dominant: who exactly is this Jesus? Jews and Gentiles, Pharisees and Sadducees—they are all trying to work it out. So Jesus takes his disciples two days' journey north for a small group retreat, and then asks the million-dollar question: 'Who do you say that I am?' (v. 15).

Their answers to a previous question (reporting others' opinions) are fascinating: Jesus is compared to those great figures who have spoken God's word, challenged Israel to be faithful and warned of imminent judgment (evidently, Jesus' preaching had not been 'meek and mild', but radical and challenging). But then Simon Peter blurts out the line: 'You are the Messiah, the Son of the living God!' It is the pivotal moment in Matthew's Gospel.

Jewish people in the first century longed for the arrival of this 'anointed' king who would restore their fortunes, perhaps re-establish their temple and fulfil God's promises. Now Simon sees this hope fulfilled before his eyes in Jesus. Importantly, he was not thereby recognising Jesus' divinity. The Messiah was expected to be a human figure, and 'son of God' had been used in the Old Testament (2 Samuel 7:14; Psalm 2:7) to describe the special status of Israel's human king in God's sight.

Even so, this is a remarkable declaration—a sign of God's revelation (v. 17). Jesus swiftly responds, giving Simon a new name (Peter means 'rock') and declaring him to be the founding member of Jesus' new community or 'assembly'—the Church. Peter's messianic confession triggers the launch of the Messiah's community, and this community, despite its failings, will reflect the Messiah's own authority and share in his victory over evil (vv. 18–19). This building—this 'temple' established by the Messiah—will not be destroyed.

This text has triggered much discussion concerning the Church and Peter's role within it. In Matthew's narrative, however, the more important questions focus on our response as readers of his Gospel. Can we make the same 'confession' about Jesus' identity, seeing him as God's anointed king over our world? The geographical setting of this story is intriguing. Within Caesarea Philippi, there was a new temple built for the worship of the Roman emperor (Caesar), who was the ruler of the entire world. Jesus, however, staying outside the city (v. 13), is hinting at an alternative truth: as Israel's Messiah-King, he (not Caesar) is the world's true Lord.

Guidelines

Our readings this week have shown us a pivotal, central period in Jesus' life. His ministry is arousing an increasing barrage of questions—whether from Jewish leaders down in Jerusalem or a Gentile woman up in Lebanon. The disciples have their own questions, too. In our final passage, however, Jesus turns the questioning back on his audience, asking them to speak out their understanding of his true identity. That can happen today. It's good to ask lots of questions of Jesus—God welcomes such honest enquiry—but eventually the tables are turned and the spotlight falls on us. The Jesus who evidently knows the dark depths of the human heart (15:19) turns to face us and invites us to get real—both about who he is and about who we are. How are we responding to his challenge?

1 A suffering Messiah

Matthew 16:21–28

After the high comes the low. Peter's key insight into Jesus' true identity (16:16) is immediately followed in Matthew's account by his being sternly rebuked by Jesus (v. 23). If you like, Peter is correct about Jesus' title but completely wrong about his job description. Peter assumes that Jesus' Messiahship means glory and political victory (as would the crowds—hence the command to keep this revelation secret: 16:20), but Jesus sees it quite differently. Effectively he has brought together two Old Testament figures (the 'messiah' and Isaiah's 'suffering servant') and conflated their roles. No one had ever done this before and it is highly paradoxical, for how can someone become king through suffering and death?

Yet Jesus insists. There is an urgent necessity about his goal (note the word 'must' in verse 21, hinting that Jesus' death will be a fulfilment of prophecy and a non-negotiable part of God's plans) and Peter's outburst cannot, and must not, get in the way. More personally, for Jesus himself this is a daunting task, a painful journey, and it will not be made any easier if his leading disciple fails to support him but instead tries to deflect him. So the Peter who, shortly before, has been the recipient of divine revelation (v. 17) is now told that he is thinking merely 'human' thoughts and is adopting the position of the evil one ('Satan': v. 23). Evidently those whom the Lord commissions can—and do—still make grave mistakes; even if we are seeking to be God's servants, we are not infallible and are ever prone to error.

Jesus goes further. What's true for him is true for his disciples. If the Messiah is going to suffer death and then be raised to life (note this clear prediction of the resurrection in v. 21, easily overlooked in these so-called 'passion predictions'), then that same pattern will hold true for his followers: the gateway to true life is through death. Jesus indicates that the worst possible outcome for human beings is that they 'forfeit their soul' (v. 26). Yet, to avoid this chilling calamity, they must paradoxically 'lose their life'. Paul will explain this paradox, teaching that repentant faith in Jesus causes our old selves effectively to be 'crucified with' Jesus—a truth then portrayed in Christian baptism (Romans 6:3–6). So, to find the new life offered by the risen Christ, we must die to self. No one can walk this road for us: as Jesus insists in this astonishing teaching, 'Whoever wants to be my disciple must… take up their cross' (v. 24). No cross, no life.

2 Transfiguration

Matthew 17:1–13

Jesus' disciples have been presented with a truth almost impossible to grasp—that the Messiah will suffer (16:21); that the exalted figure known as the 'Son of Man', who will one day 'come in his Father's glory' (16:27; see Daniel 7:13–14), will be killed. Now, six days later, the time has come for three of their number to be taken even further into this mystery. Jesus selects Peter, James and John and leads them up the side of a high mountain (probably in the foothills of Mount Hermon, to the north and east of Caesarea Philippi) for an event that will be burned into their lives for ever more (see John 1:14; 2 Peter 1:16–18).

These three were given the unique privilege of seeing the deep inner reality of Jesus, his essential and eternal 'glory'. In being 'transfigured', Jesus is revealed as one greater than both Moses (representing the Law) and Elijah (the Prophets). He is declared by a divine voice to be God's 'Son'—evidently in a much deeper sense than Peter would have meant it when he used the term (16:16). He is the one in whom God delights (v. 5) and who indeed will be raised from the dead (v. 9) but, even so, he is going to 'suffer' at human hands (v. 12).

So this extraordinary paradox remains. Some time later, Peter, James and John would be taken up another hillside (in Gethsemane, at the foot of the Mount of Olives) and there they would see this same Jesus not in solitary glory, but in lonely agony—the Lord of glory cast deep into the valley of suffering. How much we need to recognise this paradox and to be moved by what Jesus, despite his glory, did for us in going to his death.

The episode of the transfiguration contains some other key truths. Peter learns that he cannot contain God's glory, and he would do far better to stop speaking and start 'listening' to Jesus (v. 5). Above all, we see the

Father deeply affirming his Son (in word and deed), expressing his pleasure in him at a pivotal juncture in his ministry. There are lessons here for parents (how often are children told their value?) but also for all of us in relating to God as our Father. Can we truly hear these affirmative words, which God would speak to all his 'adopted' children, as being addressed to us? God wants us, as believers in his Son, to know that 'in the Beloved' we too are deeply loved (see Ephesians 1:4–6, NRSV).

3 Authority and faith

Matthew 17:14–23

Down from the mountain top—from the highs to the lows. Great experiences or moments of lucid insight and clarity are often followed by times of difficulty and confusion. Something of that pattern is seen here as Jesus and his three disciples come down from the mount of transfiguration.

For Jesus, there is the transition from a moment of glory to a need to speak again about his forthcoming suffering in Jerusalem (vv. 22–23). For the disciples, there is the rude awakening that, despite their proximity to Jesus, they currently do not have what it takes to share in his healing ministry. In a stinging rebuke, they are included in Jesus' strong condemnation of this 'unbelieving and perverse' generation (v. 17).

Yet the ultimate direction of this story is more positive: thankfully, those are not Jesus' last words on the matter, and the man's son is dramatically healed. We are seeing here, again, Jesus' own incredible authority over sickness and evil (helped by Matthew's very 'matter-of-fact' description of the healing), and also his encouragement to his disciples that they too may, in future, be able to act with similar authority. What they need, what we need, is 'faith' (vv. 20–21).

Jesus here makes a key new point. Although chiding the disciples for having only a little faith, he also makes it clear that this—only a little faith—is all that is necessary. As the saying goes, we do not need a great faith but rather faith in a great God. Our faith can be as small as 'a mustard seed' (the 'smallest' of seeds': 13:32) but, if it is faith in the God revealed in Jesus, it will be powerful in its effect—able to 'move mountains' (a dramatic image, repeated by Jesus in 21:21).

Even if Jesus' image is deliberately provocative (if taken literally), we should not duck his challenge here: we are to be those who dare to ask God for things in prayer, who do not accept the status quo but exercise faith that God can shift seemingly mountainous obstacles, who beseech him to act and are known as Jesus' disciples because, through our prayers, the life-transforming power of Jesus is released into others. What, then, are the situations—in our personal worlds and those of our family and friends—where we have too easily become resigned or defeatist and have not exercised a new, expectant faith in the power and goodness of Jesus' God?

4 The temple tax

Matthew 17:24–27
When Jesus returns to the Jewish regions of Galilee after periods in Gentile territory, he is regularly greeted by delegations from Jerusalem (see 16:1), eager to fire questions at him. This time, it is all to do with the annual two-drachma tax, levied by the Jerusalem authorities on all Jews throughout the world for the maintenance of the temple. The questioners knew that there were groups (like the Essenes at Qumran) who criticised the temple (recently rebuilt by Herod the Great, a non-Jew!) and they probably knew that Jesus had claimed both to forgive a paralysed man his sins (effectively 'bypassing' the temple as the source of forgiveness: 9:2) and to be, himself, 'greater than the temple' (12:6). So does he pay his annual temple tax, or does he see himself as somehow exempt?

The superficial, practical answer is that he does pay it (v. 25), but this year Jesus wants to make the point that, strictly, both he and Peter are exempt (v. 26). On what grounds? Jesus draws a comparison with the Roman imperial taxes (as collected by Matthew: 9:9), which are not required of Romans (the 'sons' within the family) but only of non-Romans (those 'others', outside the family, who are Rome's subjects). So, ideally, this Jewish tax should not be levied on her 'sons'. Jesus could be making the provocative and ironic point that only Gentiles should pay the tax. Almost certainly, however, he is instead making the even more provocative point that it is he himself and those who follow him who have the distinctive status of being the true 'sons'. Jesus as God's Son (16:16; 17:5) and Peter as the first member of Jesus' Church (16:18) are now in a new category. So, too, are we—and all those who exercise faith, like Peter, in Jesus as God's Messiah.

Jesus is signalling that his followers will have a new status in God's sight—and that they will not need the temple. That which the temple signified (true atonement for sins and God's presence among his people) will soon be available through other means—namely, through his own death and the gift of his Spirit in believers' lives. This year the tax will be paid as requested, but the miraculous nature of its provision (v. 27) only reveals that God is able and willing to make the benefits previously associated with the temple available to Jesus' followers in some novel ways and 'free of charge'. Do we thank God for the status we have been given as his 'children' and for the gifts of his presence and forgiveness, now brought to us directly, not through the temple, but via Jesus?

5 The value of God's children

Matthew 18:1–9

In our cultures today, with their loss of agreement about moral values, one activity is still almost universally acknowledged as evil and repugnant: taking advantage of children. When there is clear evidence of this crime, the response from others is often one of outrage. Jesus here (revealing his own love for children) connects with this outrage: his words are stern, even harrowing, but there are spiritual equivalents of child abuse, which need to be recognised as such.

Jesus has talked about 'greatness in the kingdom of heaven' (11:11), so the disciples, in their vanity, want to know how they can come out on top (see also Mark 9:33–34). Jesus takes them right back to basics, warning them that they cannot 'enter' the kingdom (let alone become the greatest within it) unless they 'become like little children'—and this requires a significant 'change' in outlook (v. 3). In Jesus' upside-down kingdom, humility is both the starting point and the route to true 'greatness'. In the words of an ancient hymn, do we have that 'true lowliness of heart that takes the humbler part'? Or are we subtly—even in our following of Jesus—motivated by some poisonous ambition?

With the child still standing in their midst, Jesus proceeds to make two further points. First, just as causing an innocent child to 'stumble' is morally repugnant, so too is the act of trying to trip up one of Jesus' followers ('those who believe in me', v. 6). In the imagery of *Pilgrim's Progress*, those who seek to entice the Christian 'pilgrim' from the true path, or to discourage them, are guilty in God's sight of the moral equivalent of child abuse and will be condemned. Jesus does not mince his words (v. 6b). He is alerting us to just how much he values his followers, and his 'zero tolerance' towards those who try to wean them away from his care. As a lioness protects her cubs, so will Jesus protect his own and deal savagely with those who interfere.

Secondly, Jesus' followers are to adopt a similarly radical approach to evil in their own lives (vv. 8–9). Jesus' graphic imagery, even if metaphorical, reflects a deep reality: sin will be judged and those who wish to 'enter life' must deal with it radically. If this hostile attitude to sin is something we must cultivate daily, then there are also times when more radical surgery is required—cutting ourselves free from a particular arena in our life that is contrary to Jesus' way. What might that be for us today?

6 A holy Church

Matthew 18:10–20

With the child still in their midst (18:2), Jesus continues to emphasise the value of these 'little ones' (expressly defined as referring to believers in Jesus: v. 6). What Jesus introduces now is not just his valuation but that of God himself—whom he tellingly describes as 'my Father in heaven' (v. 10). Jesus, as God's Son (17:5), enjoys a unique relationship with God, and believers are loved not just by God the Son but by God the Father. Even as adults, they are truly (and not just metaphorically) God's 'children'—that's why Jesus then speaks of 'your Father in heaven' (v. 14).

Jesus is introducing us here to our Father's love: as individuals, we are never beyond his loving gaze (v. 10) and are uniquely precious. Jesus then adds the picture of a solitary lost sheep. Just as God does not want a child to be tripped up and led into sin, so he does not wish one of his valued sheep to 'perish' (v. 14) and be lost to him for ever.

The point of this, though, is that we should have a radical approach to sin in our lives (18:8–9). Failure to address such sin could lead to our 'perishing'. So the wider company of Jesus' followers (the 'church', v. 17) needs also to be on its guard against this deadly poison. This leads into territory that is, to us, very uncomfortable. Is not the Church a place for forgiven sinners? Is God really looking for holiness in his Church? Do we have to confront sin in our congregations? Yet, even as we squirm, Jesus politely insists. If the church is to bear witness to the new life of Jesus' kingdom, then blatant sin should not be tolerated. Some rudimentary (but very wise) procedures are put in place (vv. 15–17)—with expulsion from the community being kept as a live option in the last resort. The early Church took these commands very seriously (see, for example, 1 Corinthians 5; 2 John 10–11). Should we not do the same?

Jesus' new community is a place where there is clarity between right and wrong, where spiritual judgments should be made, and where the values of 'heaven' are brought down to 'earth' (v. 18). And all this is because the Church is the place where Jesus, the one opposed to all sin and evil, is himself mysteriously present (v. 20). We have the Holy One in our midst—'Immanuel', 'God with us' (1:23; 28:20).

Guidelines

Our readings this week began with the verse that is commonly seen as opening the second half of Matthew's Gospel ('From that time on Jesus began...', 16:21). Now that Jesus' identity as the Messiah has been glimpsed, he can speak openly about his death, and the remainder of the Gospel will show us that inevitable journey towards Jerusalem. These chapters are, therefore, one long invitation to join with Jesus and his disciples on that journey. Are we individually ready for the journey? If so, do we accept that following Jesus will involve not only 'taking up our cross' (16:24) but also relating humbly to others who are walking along the same road? Not for nothing, then, does Jesus teach about relationships among his followers (within his 'church': 18:17), for Jesus has no 'solo' disciples. Are there any relationships in your local church that need some attention, so that together you can walk in harmony along the same path?

1 The priority of forgiveness

Matthew 18:21–35

Jesus' first words after teaching the Lord's Prayer were to explain the phrase 'forgive us our debts': 'if you do not forgive others their sins, your Father will not forgive your sins' (6:9–15). Yet just now Jesus has been talking about the importance of discipline in the life of the Church, guarding its holiness. Surely, if following Jesus is all about forgiving others, such strictness would be unnecessary? Hence, perhaps, Peter's question here on this vital topic.

In this chapter Jesus tackles head-on three of the greatest challenges for the community of his disciples: dealing with ambition and pride (v. 1), with blatant sin in ourselves and others (vv. 8–17), and with our resentments towards each other. Each challenge, if not addressed by Jesus, can become a major block, preventing us from following him effectively.

Jesus' dramatic reply to Peter (whether it is '77' or '70 x 7' times) shows the absolute priority he gives to forgiveness, and his parable explains why. If we have entered into the 'kingdom', we have entered into the service of God as our king, and this king is one who can act in one of two ways—with either severe judgment (vv. 25, 34) or extravagant mercy (v. 27). Evidently he is moved to be gracious in response to heartfelt cries for mercy (v. 26). Yet he will not allow that grace to be abused: it will be dramatically withdrawn if there is clear evidence that the cries for mercy are not heartfelt. Those who have received God's grace (for their sins against God) must exhibit the same grace towards others (who have sinned against them).

The amount of money in Jesus' parable is indeed remarkable: the wicked servant is released from a debt of millions of pounds, but extracts the last penny out of the debt to himself of just a few pounds. Jesus is teaching how vast is our debt towards God, and the utter seriousness of our sin in his sight. Perhaps we have lost sight of that? Forgiving others is never easy but, when we place our bitterness and anger towards others squarely in front of Jesus' cross, they can begin to look very small in comparison. Is there anyone today whom Jesus is calling us to forgive? Or could it be that our discipleship of Jesus has come to a halt because we are refusing to release forgiveness to someone else?

2 Sexual morality

Matthew 19:1–12

Jesus now, at last, heads south for Jerusalem, probably travelling down the eastern side of the Jordan river, en route to Jericho (20:29). Once again he is bombarded with questions. The authorities are trying to work him out: where exactly does this 'prophet' fit into their schemes? Is he liberal or conservative? Some of his answers (for example, about the purity laws: 15:10–19) suggest that he is a radical—certainly about matters of 'tradition'. Yet what about scripture itself? Will Jesus teach that the Old Testament is unreliable, perhaps even claiming that he himself is a more reliable guide?

Hence this thorny Pharisaic question about divorce, for, superficially, is there not some conflict here even within scripture? If marriage is God-given, how come Moses itemised procedures for divorce? Jesus recognises the tension but has a challenging solution: Moses' legislation did not overturn the revealed will of God in creation (see Genesis 1:26–28; 2:24) but was a concession allowed because of human 'hardness of heart'—as exemplified in these Pharisees ('your hearts were hard', v. 8). His questioners are clearly being put on the back foot!

In his answer, Jesus thus upholds the truth of scripture, seeing Genesis' teaching as coming from God himself. He affirms the goodness of our being created as male and female, and the new reality that God brings about when a husband and wife come together in marriage (creating 'one flesh'). Yet his answer explicitly recognises that sinful human beings may not be able to live up to this ideal, and his phrase 'except for sexual immorality' (v. 9) shows that he, like Moses, knows that divorce is a sad reality.

This teaching leaves us with tons of questions ('But what if…?'). The disciples were left wondering if Jesus' conservative view meant that marriage was just too demanding—better, perhaps, not to have sex at all than to be locked in a difficult marriage with no escape? That abstinence from sex was, for them, the only alternative to be envisaged is confirmed through Jesus' reply about 'eunuchs' (those unable to have marital sexual relations). Jesus and his disciples, guided by Old Testament teaching, were evidently assuming that all sex outside marriage was wrong: 'fornication' was no better than 'adultery'. What a contrast with today, when people assume that there is a convenient alternative to marriage with commitment, namely 'free' sexual relationships without commitments. Jesus' alternative vision here—his moral purity, combined with his own example of unmarried celibacy—leaves each of us aware of our own failings (and, indeed, our own 'hardness of heart'); yet it also gives us a moral compass for our lives, towards which we would do well to reorientate ourselves.

3 Attachment to wealth

Matthew 19:13–30

Jesus' journey to Jerusalem continues to attract a crowd: first, some children (where Jesus' welcoming response illustrates well his teaching about children in 18:2–6), and then a young man with a searching personal question. Jesus' clear-cut response provokes some further enquiry from the disciples—a pattern we have seen now several times before (17:19; 18:21; 19:10)—with Peter asking the crucial question.

The way Jesus responds to the rich young man is instructive. He immediately points his questioner to God himself (the source of all goodness) and to his revelation in the scriptures (the Ten Commandments). He quotes five out of the ten and adds the command 'Love your neighbour as yourself' (Leviticus 19:18), which later he will describe as the 'second' great commandment (22:39), thus summarising the Bible's teaching succinctly. Jesus is able to discern his questioner's real dilemma (his attachment to his wealth) and eventually challenges him on this point directly. He offers an invitation but leaves the man free to make his own choice. If ever people ask us genuine questions about the future directions of their lives, we would do well to follow some of Jesus' careful strategy here.

Throughout the episode, various phrases are used to describe being 'saved' (v. 25)—such as having 'eternal life', being 'perfect', or 'entering the kingdom of heaven'—but Jesus' reply indicates that the one essential route to these realities is to follow him, Jesus (v. 21). Staggeringly, as elsewhere in the Gospels, Jesus places himself at the absolute centre of God's purposes, as if to say, 'If you wish to have these things, you will now only find them through me.'

When the young man leaves, Jesus highlights the way attachment to our possessions can lure us away from following him. These words rightly challenge many of us in the Western world to ask where our true treasure lies (6:21): in the words of an old 'spiritual', would we 'rather have Jesus than anything the world affords today'? As Paul says, 'the love of money is a root of all kinds of evil' (1 Timothy 6:10), so we should be asking: what are the things that pull us away from a 'sincere and pure devotion to Christ' (2 Corinthians 11:3)? Are our hearts prone to any particular 'idols' (1 John 5:21)? Yet Jesus here also wants to encourage his followers: when tempted to complain (v. 27), we can look forward to that time when God will restore anything we have renounced here for Jesus' sake. His followers will not, in the end, be the losers.

4 The generosity of God

Matthew 20:1–16

'Many who are last will be first' (19:30). Jesus' puzzling words, designed to encourage his disciples, need some explanation, so Matthew now includes an extended parable of Jesus (similar in length to the three parables in chapter 25), which explains how this can be. Within God's 'kingdom' there are some surprises, and things do not always turn out as human beings would expect. This is because God's values are different from those of human society but also, as it turns out, because God is a God of surprising 'generosity' (v. 15).

God is like a landowner who wants people to be gainfully employed on his estate but then pays them, at the end of day, an equal amount, regardless of how many hours they have worked. We can sense the shock of those labourers who toiled throughout the 'heat of the day' only to receive the same amount as those who started work in the late afternoon. Yet they, and we, need to reckon with God's grace. None of the things we receive from God's hand can be seen as our 'rights'—what we have deserved—but only as a free gift of God's generosity. We must not begrudge his generosity to others, because we depend entirely on that same generosity for what we ourselves receive.

There was a warning here—in the days of Jesus and of Matthew—that the nation of Israel might begrudge God's generosity going out to include the Gentiles. Much of Jesus' teaching in these chapters touches on this vital issue, hinting that God's kingdom, as a result of Jesus' work, is about to break open to the whole world (see, for example, 21:43; 28:19). Yet there was also a warning to Jesus' disciples that they might start to see themselves as having a 'first' or prior claim on God's grace through their following of Jesus—only to discover that Jesus wants many others to find that grace, too.

This applies also to us today: the risen Jesus is perennially warning his followers—those who have experienced his grace—that that grace does not stop with them but needs to be shared with others. So long as we think of ourselves as the 'last' to deserve God's grace, there is the promise that we may become 'first'; but if ever we think of ourselves as 'first', there is the warning that we may become 'last'. Are there ways in which we are becoming presumptuous of God's grace?

5 A mother's request

Matthew 20:17–23

Jesus is travelling southwards along the Jordan valley towards Jericho, bound eventually for Jerusalem (v. 17). Now, for the third time, he explains to his twelve disciples that the journey will end in his death—this time explicitly mentioning his being 'crucified' (v. 19).

There is, therefore, something quite shocking about the arrival of the mother of James and John with her ill-timed and selfish request that they be given prime seats at the messianic banquet—the time when Jesus is given his 'kingdom'. No doubt she (perhaps along with most of the others in Jesus' entourage) imagined that Jesus would be setting up a royal dynasty in Jerusalem and establishing an independent Jewish kingdom there, free from pagan domination. Hence Jesus' need to spell out three times his quite different agenda. Hence, too, his stern reply to this request, which has arisen out of pure ignorance (v. 22).

Jesus begins by speaking about the 'cup' that he must drink. The Old Testament prophets used this imagery to speak of the 'cup of God's wrath'; they saw it as being given to God's enemies, causing them to stagger as they drained God's judgment 'to the dregs' (Psalm 75:8; Isaiah 51:17–23). Jesus is evidently viewing his forthcoming death in a similar way—as a drinking of God's judgment—and that is why he will use the 'cup' imagery again in Gethsemane (26:39). Jesus has a lonely, bitter calling.

This makes the mother's request even more impertinent and out of place, and Jesus immediately highlights the fact that they are talking at cross purposes. In fact, her request goes badly wrong. Jesus announces that James and John will share in his 'cup'—presumably in the lesser sense of suffering for God's sake—but that only God can apportion the prime seats in the kingdom.

There are warnings here of the ways in which we may make inappropriate requests of God in prayer, or may try to squeeze Jesus into our own agendas. What have we been praying for recently, which deep down really reflects our pride and selfishness? Despite our familiarity with the story of Jesus' crucifixion, have we grasped the full extent of what Jesus was doing on the cross—'bearing our sins' and removing God's judgment (1 Peter 2:24)? Jesus reveals here some of the burden placed upon him as he approached the cross; so we, his followers, should view his death with a similar seriousness, not undervaluing it.

6 A countercultural kingdom

Matthew 20:24–34

Imagine the scene around the campfire that night, when the ten other disciples discover what James and John have been up to! They are incensed and 'indignant' (v. 24) at this shameless opportunism. Part of their indignation, no doubt, is well motivated, but some of it might be a subtle means of covering over the fact that, if they were honest, they too would have liked to ask for the prime seats in Jesus' kingdom. So now they take the opportunity to express their disdain at the brothers and distance themselves publicly from such ambition. We ourselves need to note this device in the human heart—whereby we sometimes reserve our severest criticism for the actions of others that we identify and fear in ourselves.

Jesus recognises this and calls all twelve together for an urgent team meeting (v. 25). They have been arguing about who should be 'first' among them, so now Jesus teaches them that the route towards that goal is the path of service, even slavery (vv. 26–27). Jesus' kingdom is indeed one with upside-down values. Throughout human history it will stand in sharp contrast to other kingdoms, where rulers use their authority to 'lord' it over their subjects, dominating them from a perspective of pride and power. Those who want to follow Jesus, by contrast, must develop a counter-cultural mindset, actively seeking a lowly and humble heart.

The inspiration for this humility comes from considering Jesus' own example: though he was the exalted and glorious Son of Man, he came into the world to 'serve' others; more than that, he will shortly 'give his life as a ransom for many' (v. 28). Again we see how consumed and focused Jesus is, as he approaches Jerusalem on his journey to the cross. And, again, we need to hear Jesus' own understanding of the purpose of his death and let it dictate to us how we should understand it. Jesus is giving the most costly gift (his own life) to purchase our freedom from slavery (the word 'ransom' picks up the Old Testament imagery of God 'redeeming' his people—that is, buying them back to himself, thus bringing them freedom).

Motivated by the cross, the Christian community needs to embody these countercultural values, yet human pride so often prevents us from doing it. Importantly, Jesus is not saying that his community should have no due patterns of authority established within it. Authority and leadership are vital aspects of a healthy community, but the hallmark of all Christian leaders is to be humility and readiness to serve. How true is that of us?

Guidelines

Our readings from Matthew's Gospel come to an end, for now, with a moving scene of two blind men being healed: 'Lord, we want our sight.' Jesus touches their eyes with 'compassion' and they are healed (20:29–34). The Jesus we follow is one with both power and compassion, and this should cause us, like the blind men, to get up on our feet and 'follow him' on the road. Are there any ways, however, in which we have got stuck in our following of Christ, where we have, effectively, come to a standstill and stopped moving forward? If so, this may be because there is something in our lives that we urgently need to bring to Jesus' attention—something that, if not addressed, will cause us to remain languishing by the roadside. Bringing such things to Christ requires courage but we should be encouraged by his gracious invitation to us: 'What do you want me to do for you?' Jesus wants to hear an honest answer to that question from each one of us.

Psalms 26 (25)—37 (36)

The psalms are the prayers of Israel. Some of them may have been composed by David; some are older, while many reflect the spirit and prayer life of Israel in later times. They are prayers with which Jesus, his family and his disciples would have been intimately familiar. In the prayer tradition of the Church, they are seen as spoken by Christ himself, prayed by him in the name of his followers who form the body of Christ. Thus, in reflecting on them and in praying them, we enter into Christ's spirituality in a special way.

This is the third group of twelve psalms to be covered over two weeks' reading. In the reflections, some topics will already have been the subject of meditation in previous issues of *Guidelines*. I hope I have avoided the twin dangers of boring repetition and of unfeeling neglect of important themes expressed in these psalms.

All the psalms have a sort of rubric or stage-direction at the beginning, which is not part of the psalm. These titles were added later and have dubious historical value. Each of the psalms in this group, except 33 (32), has 'Of David' as part of its title. Sometimes the psalms are even placed at some particular moment in David's life. So Psalm 34 (33) is said to have been 'when David feigned madness'—that is, to show the Philistine king that he was not a danger (1 Samuel 21:11–16). It may be helpful to picture David as praying them.

These notes are based on the Revised Grail Psalter and, unless otherwise stated, on the New Jerusalem Bible.

A note on numbering: The Revised Grail Psalter, in accordance with the Roman Catholic tradition, uses the numbering of the Greek version of the Psalms, rather than the Hebrew. In the Greek text, the Hebrew Psalms 9 and 10 are shown as a single psalm—Psalm 9. Thus the Greek version stays one number behind until Psalm 148. Because many Protestant versions adopt the Hebrew numbering (following Luther's preference), however, both numbers have been given in psalm references between 10 and 147. You will find the Hebrew number given first, with the Greek in brackets afterwards.

1 Give judgment for me, O Lord

Psalm 26 (25)

Let us begin with two easy misconceptions. This psalm is often regarded as a sort of entry liturgy, pronounced by someone coming to pray in the temple (perhaps at one of the great feasts), declaring his innocence on the threshold and his intention of cleansing his hands in innocence at the washing-fountain which presumably stood at the entrance to the temple— as it does now at the entrance to the Muslim Dome of the Rock, which occupies the position of the temple in Jerusalem. This scenario is unlikely, for in the Bible there are no instructions for such a ceremony and no evidence that it ever occurred. Nevertheless, some of us may find it helpful to imagine such a situation.

The second misconception is that the psalm is a complacent protestation of innocence, such as the self-satisfied Pharisee would have made in Luke's parable of the Pharisee and the tax collector (Luke 18:9–14). No, the psalmist is not complacent. Yes, he does protest his innocence, but there are redeeming features.

Firstly, he is very much aware that he is still on the road: 'I have walked in my integrity' (v. 1 and again in v. 11, a nice bracket), 'I walk according to your truth' (v. 3), and 'My foot stands on level ground' (v. 12). This is all reminiscent of the letter to the Hebrews 4:1–11, which insists that the Christian is still on pilgrimage and has not yet entered the place of rest which was promised at the end of the exodus wanderings.

Secondly, there is an appeal for redemption (v. 11). This image is often and aptly used to describe Christ's work (also called salvation, reconciliation and other images). The basic idea behind it is release from slavery. It often stands for buying back hostages or captives. In the Bible it usually refers to the Lord releasing his people from slavery in Egypt, purchasing them as slaves are purchased and making them his own people, to serve him alone. So the psalmist is praying that he may be released and purchased in the same way.

Thirdly, there is an appeal to the covenant of mercy. Verse 3 speaks of 'mercy' and 'truth', that pair of words which sets every bell of love and fidelity ringing. God's 'mercy' is his love, *hesed*—a family love, a forgiving love, the very definition of God's nature. And God's 'truth' is his truthfulness, in the sense of his fidelity to the promises he has made, which will never fail. We rely on this truthfulness for all his promises. It is the bedrock of Paul's letter to the Romans. It is the idea fulfilled in Jesus, the true shepherd, the true vine, the way, the truth and life. The psalmist is not complacent but reliant.

2 The Lord is my light and my salvation

Psalm 27 (26)

It is possible to argue that this psalm is formed from two psalms joined together, verses 1–6 and 7–14. The earlier half is more optimistic and confident, the later more threatened. On the other hand, there is a continuity of thought. Either this shows that the psalm is a single composition or it gives the reason why two disparate psalms were joined together! The idea of seeking the Lord is prominent in both parts (vv. 4, 8). The longing is similarly expressed: 'all the days of my life to gaze on the beauty of the Lord' (v. 4) and to 'see the Lord's goodness in the land of the living' (v. 13). In both parts there is a threat from enemies or foes (vv. 2, 6, 11). Who these foes are, we cannot know, but the images of threats facing the psalmist are so varied in the psalms that there is no need to deduce that actual warfare with an army (v. 3) is envisaged.

The striking feature of the psalm is the ardent desire to be with the Lord, to dwell in the shelter of his tent, to see his face, to live in the house of the Lord 'all the days of my life'. 'Though father and mother forsake me' (v. 10) is very forceful. The intensity of God's love is often compared to a father's or a mother's love, and we must remember that this is in a Jewish context, where a united and loving family is of paramount importance. Who can describe the emotional trauma of any mother abandoning her baby? And the parable of the prodigal son shows how Jesus sees the intensity of a father's love. That father and mother should both forsake a child is an unthinkable disaster, and yet the Lord will be there to receive me if that disaster should occur.

Corresponding to this warmth of relationship is the constant physical imagery of the psalm—gazing on the Lord's beauty, seeing the Lord's goodness, seeking the Lord's face, under the cover of his tent, within his tent. All of these phrases bespeak a sort of physical intimacy with the Lord.

3 To you, O Lord, I call

Psalm 28 (27)

Here we are really confronted with the issue of the use of the Psalms! It is not easy to follow the sequence of thought in this psalm on the assumption that it is all spoken by one suppliant. If we take seriously the idea that the Psalms were all used for some part of the liturgy of the temple, we can divide this one into four sections, representing an interplay between two speakers:

vv. 1–4   An individual lament, begging for release from persecution.
v. 5   Reassurance pronounced by a representative of the temple.
vv. 6–7   Praise and thanksgiving by the original suppliant.
vv. 8–9   A final, more general blessing by the representative of the temple.

It is also suggested, from verse 8, that the speaker is the king, the 'anointed', unless this term is to be related closely to the people of the Lord (v. 9), who are also an anointed people.

Perhaps this is a psalm in which the Christian must principally rejoice in the progress of revelation, for Christian spirituality surpasses that of the psalm on three points. Firstly, the finality of going down into 'the pit' (v. 1) no longer obtains: for the Christian, death is not a blank ending, a descent into the grim world of Sheol, but a door through which we all pass towards eternal life. Secondly, the thirst for payback and vengeance (vv. 3–5) is not part of a Christian mentality, since Jesus taught so repeatedly that there is no place for revenge but only for the joy of forgiveness, for not only 'vertically' receiving the forgiveness of God but also for 'horizontally' sharing it with others. Thirdly, the Lord is indeed a saving refuge for his anointed (v. 8), since he vindicated and exalted his Anointed One, Jesus, and with Jesus takes up all his anointed ones who share in the body of Christ.

4 Ascribe to the Lord glory and strength!

Psalm 29 (28)

This noble psalm in praise of God is built on a sharp contrast. It begins and ends (vv. 1–2, 10–11) with the calm of heaven, where the 'heavenly powers' (themselves gods and goddesses of myth) reverence the Lord. Within this envelope comes the turmoil on earth provoked by the Lord's powerful action. It is in the form of a victory song, like Miriam's victory song in the exodus after the crossing of the Reed Sea (Exodus 15:1–18), celebrating the Lord's strength and the glory of his name (v. 2).

Several features of the psalm are drawn from the Canaanite culture that Israel found on entering the promised land. The rhythm is characteristic of Canaanite poetry. Three times occurs the figure, typical of Canaanite poetry, consisting of two lines parallel with a third element added (1, 2 // 1, 2, 3). So we have 'The Lord's voice on the waters, the Lord on the waters in quantity' (v. 3), then 'The Lord's voice shatters the cedars, the Lord shatters the cedars of Lebanon' (v. 5), and finally 'The Lord's voice shakes the wilderness, the Lord shakes the wilderness of Kadesh' (v. 8). The most powerful things in nature are shattered. The Israelites were daunted by the sea and pictured it as an uncontrollable sea-monster. The majestic cedars of Lebanon tower and spread in their might. The huge Mount Hermon ('Sirion' is the Phoenician name) is made to heave and bound. The Greek version of verse 6b reads 'like a young rhinoceros' instead of 'like a young wild ox', and it is hard to think of anything in the animal kingdom less bouncy than a rhinoceros. The Lord, meanwhile, sits majestically enthroned over the flood (v. 10)—in local mythology, another goddess of the chaotic and dreaded sea.

It has even been held that this psalm was originally a Canaanite prayer addressed to their god, Baal, and that it was simply taken over, with the substitution of the name 'the Lord' for 'Baal'. Baal was a storm-god who made his presence and power known in storm and lightning; he was often represented as standing on a bull and hurling a thunderbolt. In the Bible, the visitation of the Lord is often described in similar terms of thunder and earthquake, derived from Israel's experience of the Lord on Sinai and in the wilderness of Kadesh. In this psalm there is the same turmoil in nature, but provoked by the more majestic and intangible voice of the Lord, which strikes seven times (the number of perfection) in the course of the psalm. From this throne the Lord effortlessly controls nature and gives strength and power to his people.

5 I will thank you, Lord, for you have drawn me up

Psalm 30 (29)

This is an attractive little prayer of thanksgiving for rescue from death. The thanks of the first three verses set the scene. All other biblical instances of the word translated 'drawn me up' are of water drawn up in a bucket from a well or a river: the psalmist has been drawn up like water from a well. This also fits the idea of being lifted from Sheol or the pit, for, until the idea of resurrection life became clear, death was envisaged as the descent into a grim and powerless half-life among similar shades. No strength there even to praise the Lord! At the arrival of the king of Babylon, the shades would rise up from the powerlessness of their thrones, only to sink back down again into their impotence (Isaiah 14:9–11).

In the main part of the psalm (bracketed by 'sing psalms' and 'thanks' in both verses 4 and 12), the psalmist does not explain in what the threat of death consisted. He only makes clear that his complacent self-confidence in being 'like a mountain fastness' was shattered, replaced by a helpless plea for the Lord's loving mercy. He seems almost to have challenged the Lord: 'Can dust give you praise or proclaim your faithfulness?' (v. 9) Was this a military, a moral or a medical crisis? At any rate, there was a pretty sharp conversion from self-reliance to reliance on the Lord, expressed in the sackcloth of repentance.

It is difficult to envisage the circumstances of the original use of this psalm in the temple. Later tradition associates it with thanksgiving for the deliverance of the temple from desecration at the time of the Maccabean persecution (167–164BC). Whatever the original circumstances, the frank, personal and joyful tone makes it a lovely prayer for any occasion when one's own self-assurance, mental, physical or moral, has been stripped away and one is forced to throw oneself cheerfully on to the mercy of God's own bucket-lift.

6 In you, O Lord, I take refuge

Psalm 31 (30)

This lament is puzzling, with two puzzles in particular. The first is that it seems to be a tissue of sentiments that occur elsewhere in the Bible (including the Psalms). Commentators call these 'conventional formulae'. It is as though the composer of the psalm, not wanting to use his own language, had culled them elsewhere and brought them all together. Rather than listing all the 'conventional formulae', I simply draw attention to the close similarity between the first two verses and the opening of Psalm 71 (70), and between verse 13 and Jeremiah 20:10. Most of the other instances could be explained as merely the conventional language and imagery of distress.

The second puzzle concerns the sudden change from lament to thanksgiving, and arises from our ignorance of the liturgical context and use of the psalms. Ought we to assume a certain amount of action in the background to the texts? Is a liturgical procession for the entry of the ark into the temple the background of Psalm 24 (23)? In Psalm 28 (27), is there a real dialogue between a suppliant and a representative of the temple? In our present psalm (and correspondingly in others), should we assume the intervention of a blessing after verse 18, which turns the suppliant from lament to thanksgiving?

The structure of the first part of the psalm may be understood as a chiasmus:

vv. 1–5: Confident prayer for help
    vv. 6–8: Declaration of trust in the Lord
        vv. 9–13: Lament
    vv. 14–15: Declaration of trust in the Lord
vv. 16–18: Confident prayer for deliverance

This is followed by the thanks and praise of verses 19–24.

One precious feature is verse 5, placed by Luke (23:46) as Jesus' last words on the cross. Mark 15:34 and Matthew 27:46 give the intonation of Psalm 22, implying that the message of the triumph of God and the vindication of the sufferer is the lesson of that whole dire scene. The Gospel of John has a very different scene (19:26–27), in which Jesus founds the first Christian community by joining together Mary and the beloved disciple, upon whom he breathes forth his Spirit.

Luke's interpretation brings to a close the great scene in which Jesus concludes his whole mission of bringing God's forgiveness to the world. He forgives his executioners and welcomes the repentant 'thief' into his kingdom. After that, he himself voluntarily entrusts his life to his Father, and the scene ends with the general repentance of the bystanders. Such a peaceful description of the ending of a tumultuous and galling story was much valued by the Hellenistic audiences for which Luke wrote.

Guidelines

With the exception of the magnificent Psalm 29 (28), this group of psalms comprises personal prayers of petition, pronounced in various situations of need. We cannot now tell to what extent they were integrated into the liturgical action of the temple. Were they part of it, or did the suppliant simply go and ask an official to hand out a suitable psalm for prayer on each particular occasion? Even in deep need, the suppliant is always confident of the Lord's help, and usually during the recitation of the psalm itself, for one psalm after another ends with a prayer of praise and thanksgiving.

For the Christian, the circumstances of prayer have changed. We may find ourselves surrounded by liars, evil plots, scorn of neighbours and malicious gossip, but an army encamped against us and the threat of Sheol are less likely to menace us. In prayer we are, perhaps, more conscious of threats from within, from our own faults, failures and limitations. However, all these threats may be applied as images of our own peculiar devils, and function equally well as stimuli to prayer and petition. Similarly, the confident thanksgiving for the Lord's help may serve to express our confident gratitude that the Lord will deliver us from these enemies.

1 Blessed the sinner whose offence is forgiven

Psalm 32 (31)

This was St Augustine's favourite psalm. As he lay dying, he had it written on the wall where he could see it and reflect upon it for encouragement. Like all psalms that begin with the promise 'Blessed is…', it has a Wisdom element, but the dominant characteristic is joy in the frank confession of sin.

The first part (vv. 3–5) lays out the story of guilt. At first I pretend that nothing is wrong. I hide my guilt even from myself, almost convincing myself. But the discomfort and strain become too great, and I may recognise that the firm hand of God is pressing upon me till I can no longer evade the pressure. As soon as I decide to acknowledge my sin ('I will confess'—future), the guilt has already (past tense) been forgiven. God demands no long or tortuous process. That was how Jesus went out to tax collectors, sinners, prostitutes, scribes and Pharisees, and drew them into God's forgiveness, not conditionally on their first changing their ways or even promising to amend. Jesus did not interrogate the woman who was a sinner about her intentions (Luke 7:36–51). 'I am to stay at your house today,' he said to Zacchaeus when Zacchaeus had only shown curiosity, not repentance (Luke 19:1–5). It is enough that I should respond to the touch of God's hand by admitting that I am myself the real source of the trouble. Immediately God becomes a hiding-place, a place of safety and refuge, 'with cries of deliverance' (v. 7).

After this personal and intimate self-revelation, there follows a short didactic section in a different rhythm and the imaged Wisdom style (vv. 8–10), using the lively figure of harnessing a stubborn mount. It is difficult to know who the speaker and the recipient, the 'I' and the 'you', are. Is God assuring the repentant sinner of continued guidance, or is the latter sharing what he has learnt with others? The warmth and tenderness of the previous section is continued in the idea of being surrounded by God's loving mercy, linked back to being surrounded by cries of deliverance (v. 7). Finally the psalmist simply breaks out into cries of joy.

2 The word of the Lord

By the first three verses, this psalm is firmly established as a song of joyful triumph. The last word of verse 3 clinches it: *teru'ah* means a fanfare or battle cry, an acclamation or cry of victory—in any case, noisy and celebratory. What is being celebrated?

The first part of the psalm (vv. 4–12) celebrates the creation, how the world was brought into being by the word of the Lord. The second part concentrates on the Lord's continuing oversight of the world, as he watches or gazes on the world and we wait for the final revelation of his faithful love. Any possibility that the Lord is a mere control-freak is excluded by this envelope of the concept of faithful love (vv. 5, 22). On the contrary, God's direction of the world is an expression of his faithful and fatherly love for his people, that brilliant word *hesed*, which designates the unbreakable reciprocal love of family members towards one another. This is the unfailing love that God has promised to his people.

The first part of this triumphant celebration dwells on the creation narrative, where God 'spoke and it came into being', circling round three concepts: the spreading out of the heavens (v. 6), the gathering together of the waters (v. 7), and the firm establishment of the earth and its peoples (v. 8). God's design is supreme and unalterable. For the Christian, this whole idea is enriched and reaches its fullness by the designation of Jesus as the incarnate Word of God (John 1:1–18), who brings creation to its completion and in whom creation reaches its zenith (Ephesians 1:10, the climax of the great hymn of God's plan). Christ is the *logos* of God's design, the master-plan personified, who gives sense, order and direction to the whole of creation.

The celebration is not, however, confined to the act of creation in the 'Big Bang' aeons ago, for the second half of the psalm relates to God's continuing work of creation as he watches over the world. No king and his army, no horse and its strength (note the neat parallels of verses 16 and 17) can disturb God's designs. All is directed towards the outworking of God's *hesed* for his people (vv. 18, 22), and issues in the same joy with which the psalm began. The final mention of 'waiting for the Lord' (v. 20) directs Christian attention to the prophecy of the eschatological city of

God, the new Jerusalem (Revelation 21—22), the final consummation for which we are waiting.

3 Taste and see that the Lord is good

Psalm 34 (33)

This is an acrostic psalm in the Wisdom tradition, and its formal data are easily summarised. Each verse begins with a successive letter of the Hebrew alphabet (only one being omitted, and one verse added at the end of the series), which gives the psalm a certain, not unpleasant, stiffness of expression. The parallelism of the pairs of lines is very pronounced, sometimes in the same direction (for example, v. 3), sometimes in opposite directions (for example, v. 9). After the extended and joyful invitation to praise the Lord (vv. 1–8), the didactic or Wisdom part begins, gently giving rules for good conduct.

The chief burden of the teaching is to revere or fear the Lord (vv. 7, 9, 11). Fear and reverence are not particularly modern virtues. In a man-to-man (or woman-to-woman) society, we pride ourselves on standing tall and independent from anyone, not cringing before any potentate or authority. Precisely! God is not anyone. By no stretch of the imagination can we stand proud before God. In a wonderful poem, Isaiah describes the only due reaction to God, 'Go into the rock, hide in the dust, in terror of the Lord, at the brilliance of his majesty, when he arises to make the earth quake' (Isaiah 2:10). This is why the sacred/scary intimate name of the Lord, YHWH, is never pronounced. In his vocation experience of the Lord in the temple, Isaiah cringes as unclean before the Holy One of Israel (6:5). St Augustine describes his awe before this daunting presence: '*inhorresco et inardesco*', 'I burn with longing, but the hairs on the nape of my neck stand on end'. 'Perfect love drives out fear,' we are told (1 John 4:18), but only one sort of fear, and we must never lose our awed reverence at our incomparability to God.

The optimism of the moral teaching of this psalm may seem excessive at a surface level. The Christian believes that the Lord will eventually rescue the righteous from all their distress (v. 17), but not necessarily in this world. It is a hope that sustains us in the long run. However, there are times when we find that Job's anger and protests at his inexplicable suffering chime in more fittingly with our own feelings.

We cannot understand why we should suffer so much while the wicked get off scot-free. This is where Job's awe at his final experience of the wisdom and power of the Lord comes in. We cannot question God's plan; we can only accept it in consciousness of our own limitations.

4 Take up your buckler and shield

Psalm 35 (34)

In reflecting on this psalm, asking for strength and victory against opponents, the first question to ask is what sort of opponents are envisaged. There is plenty of military language—buckler, shield, javelin, spear—but there is also other imagery: the opponents are like lions; they are to be like chaff in the wind, their path a slippery slope. The predominant imagery is, however, of the law courts. The opening plea is expressed in terms of strife at law, and ideas compatible with this recur constantly: lying witnesses, asking questions, shame, mockery, vindication and disgrace, rather than wounds, blood and death. Military imagery can be more easily used in a legal situation than legal imagery in a military situation. The betrayal by the friend whom the psalmist supported during sickness (vv. 12–14) also fits this legal scene better.

For the purposes of our own prayer, however, an appeal for justice in the law courts is of little use. We know only too well that, in many ways, we are far from innocent before the Lord. Personally I find little appeal in the solution of imagining the enemies as devils or temptations: it is too easy to personify in this way my own evil tendencies, as though they, and not I, were responsible for my frequent failures. I prefer, therefore, to concentrate on, and pray about, the concepts of divine justice and salvation.

In ordinary language, if I cry out for justice, I want to set right something that is wrong. Someone who is 'brought to justice' is normally punished. When 'justice is done', it is normally vengeance. Justice occurs in function of law. In the Bible, also, justice is in function of Law, but it is God's Law, given to Israel, and this makes a total difference. God's Law is God's revelation, enabling us to imitate God, to live as the image of God and in harmony with God. It is the furtherance of the promises to Abraham that God would protect him and make his offspring like the sand on the seashore. So it is a saving justice, in accord with God's saving generosity, not giving us our deserved punishment but precisely rescuing us from our deserts. So Isaiah can say, 'My saving justice will last for ever and my salvation for all generations' (51:8). In the same way, Paul can appeal to God's saving justice (sometimes translated 'righteousness'). We are rescued from punishment by God's saving justice, simply by trusting in that saving justice.

5 Your mercy, O Lord, reaches to heaven

Psalm 36 (35)

This psalm is often contrasted with Psalm 1, which characterises first the friend of God (like a well-watered tree) and then the evildoer (like chaff before the wind). This psalm does somewhat the same in reverse, first reflecting on the complacent and godless evildoer ('his words are mischief and deceit', v. 3), then rejoicing in God's generous mercy ('in your light we see light', v. 9). Verses 5–10 are more a celebration of God's mercy than a prayer for it, though such a prayer is of course implied.

However, this celebration of God's mercy provokes us to continue the reflections of the previous psalm on God's saving justice, since God's righteousness and his mercy are strongly similar concepts. In the central section, God's mercy is mentioned three times, God's justice or righteousness twice, and God's truth or fidelity also. After the first breaking of the covenant on Mount Sinai, God's nature, the meaning of the divine name YHWH, was revealed to Moses as mercy and forgiveness (Exodus 34:6–7); so these three concepts circle round the same idea. God is true to the divine nature and to the divine Law revealed on Sinai precisely by being merciful and by forgiving. For us sinners, therefore, this is life and light: 'in your light we see light'. The friend of God is not so much the person who acts blamelessly as one who turns to God and puts all trust in the divine forgiveness.

Such an attitude may well produce the occasional good action, too! As the letter of James challenges, 'So you have faith and I have good deeds?

Show me this faith of yours without deeds, then! It is by my deeds that I will show you my faith' (2:18). However, the difference between the evil-doer and the friend of God consists in the attitude: really determined evil-doers are satisfied and complacent in their own plots and self-absorption, whereas those 'of upright heart' put all their trust outside themselves, in God's mercy, forgiveness and saving justice.

6 Do not fret because of the wicked

Psalm 37 (36)

This is a fine example of a Wisdom psalm, built on an alphabetical framework. In the Hebrew, the structure is quite regular, each pair of lines beginning with a successive letter of the alphabet. In the translation, nearly all of these pairs come out as a quatrain, though occasionally in three or five lines. As a Wisdom psalm, it is built on the conventional Hebrew teaching that the moral life brings its own reward—in the end. God rewards those who are faithful to him and his teachings.

But does he? This simplistic morality seems to be built on a system of rewards and punishments in this life. Does honesty really pay? Practical experience teaches that this is not, in fact, the case. There are enough successful sharks around to call into question the comfortable assertion, 'A little longer and the wicked one is gone' (v. 10). The Bible itself questions this teaching massively in the book of Job, where Job doggedly retains his loyalty to God even though he feels himself hounded and tortured by God. No less, the book of Qoheleth (Ecclesiastes) questions all the assumptions about happiness in this life. What, then, of the simple morality of the Beatitudes, which echoes so many verses here? 'The humble shall own the land' (v. 11; Matthew 5:4)? They don't. Must we rely on pie in the sky as a reward for drudgery in this life?

No Christian who prays this psalm can limit the prayer to such bargain-morality. Nor does this psalm itself. Such a relationship to God would be about as successful as a marriage undertaken so that each partner could get as much as possible out of the other. Our relationship to God must be one of getting to know the Lord more and more profoundly and intimately, and being more and more ready to sacrifice ourselves for the beloved. If there is love, a mother delights in the chores of motherhood, and spouse delights in caring for spouse. Lovers will put up with anything as long as they can stay together. The most wearisome or demeaning task undertaken for the beloved becomes a joy. So in the psalm there is a companionship and love that goes beyond a mere bargain: 'Be still before the Lord and wait in patience' (v. 7). The only factor that counts is joy in the relationship. If truly 'the Law of God is in his heart' (v. 31), then prosperity and adversity take second place.

Guidelines

With the partial exception of Psalm 33 (32) on the word of the Lord in creation, all the psalms in this group reflect on our current life and behaviour. There is no relief of historical psalms about the past or messianic psalms about the future. This yields a fairly intense and testing group of meditations, in which we need to examine ourselves and our motivations, our relationships with God and with the world. They have been Wisdom psalms, emerging from the rich tradition of Near Eastern Wisdom, but enhanced by Israel's closeness to and covenant relationship with God. This tradition will be enhanced still more by revelation in Christ, which brings us to a deeper understanding of so many themes in human life. Thus we can pray these psalms in the spirit in which they were composed; but, if we pray them in the light of the New Testament revelation, they are yet richer and more rewarding.

Don't forget to renew your annual subscription to *Guidelines*! If you enjoy the notes, why not also consider giving a gift subscription to a friend or local minister?

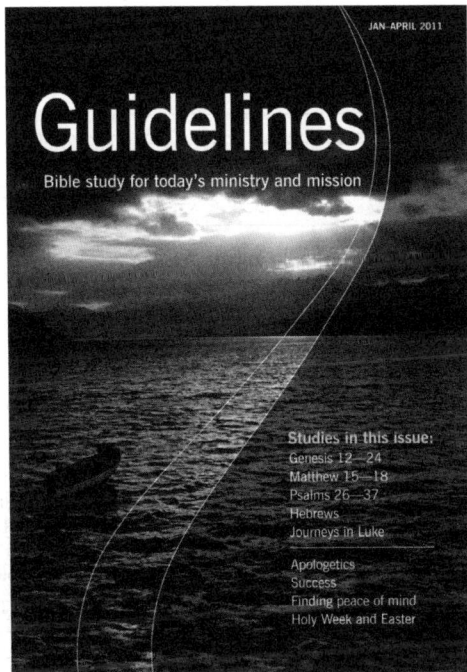

You will find a subscription order form overleaf.
Guidelines is also available from your local Christian bookshop.

SUBSCRIPTIONS

❏ I would like to take out a subscription myself (complete your name and address details only once)

❏ I would like to give a gift subscription (please complete both name and address sections below)

Your name _____

Your address _____

_____ Postcode _____

Tel _____ Email _____

Gift subscription name _____

Gift subscription address _____

_____ Postcode _____

Gift message (20 words max.) _____

_____

Please send *Guidelines* beginning with the May 2011 / September 2011 / January 2012 issue: (delete as applicable)

(please tick box)	UK	SURFACE	AIR MAIL
GUIDELINES	❏ £14.70	❏ £16.50	❏ £19.95
GUIDELINES 3-year sub	❏ £36.90		
GUIDELINES pdf version	❏ £11.70 (UK and overseas)		

Confirm your email address _____

Please complete the payment details below and send, with appropriate payment, to: **BRF, 15 The Chambers, Vineyard, Abingdon OX14 3FE.**

Total enclosed £ _____ (cheques should be made payable to 'BRF')

Please charge my Visa ❏ Mastercard ❏ Switch card ❏ with £ _____

Card no. ☐☐☐☐ ☐☐☐☐ ☐☐☐☐ ☐☐☐☐ ☐☐☐☐

Expires ☐☐☐☐ Security code ☐☐☐

Issue no (Switch only) ☐☐☐☐

Signature (essential if paying by credit/Switch) _____

BRF is a Registered Charity

Hebrews

Hebrews is one of the richest, most dense but also most pastorally meaningful books in the Bible. It is not always an easy read, mainly because it is deeply embedded in its particular cultural context, which is not our own. It seems to have been written to address the concerns and anxieties of a very particular set of people. At one level, their difficulties were not unique—pressure from the society around them, suffering, and the danger of simply 'drifting away'—and so we can benefit from overhearing the warnings and encouragements they received. However, they were facing a specific problem, for its original readers seem to have been Jews at the time when there was a 'parting of the ways' between Jews who believed in Jesus and those who did not. (I shall refer to the latter belief throughout as 'traditional Judaism'.) For those who did believe in Jesus, their religious mindset and expectations had been set by their life within traditional Judaism, yet now they were estranged from it. They had accepted Jesus as the Jewish Messiah—their Messiah—yet now their loyalty to him was cutting them off from the temple and its sacrifices. Without the sacrificial system, how could sin be dealt with and relationship with God maintained? Had they chosen wrongly? Did the scriptures support their choice?

Thus we have to accept that, in part, Hebrews is answering questions that may not seem immediately relevant to us. Nevertheless, in responding to those questions, the writer explores significant issues in both pastoral theology and scriptural exegesis. An added twist to this context is that the writer seems to be using the Greek translation of the Old Testament, not the Hebrew, as his Bible; also, when he talks about the sacrificial system, he does so on the basis of the biblical texts, not what was really going on in Jerusalem. This suggests that its context is diaspora Judaism—Jews in the wider Roman Empire, not in or around the land of Israel itself. The letter is probably best dated to AD60–70, before the destruction of the temple in Jerusalem (for that would have so greatly supported the writer's arguments, it is impossible to imagine that he wouldn't have mentioned it), but after a sense of 'parting of the ways' had started to gain momentum. Strictly speaking, the letter is anonymous (there has been much speculation about its author over the years). Nevertheless, this might lead to a misunderstanding, for those reading the text knew perfectly well who it was by (see 13:18). It was a genuine letter but, since it was carried by hand and read out in the church, there was no need to write on the paper who it was by (just as my sermon texts don't have my name on them).

Quotations are taken from the New Revised Standard Version of the Bible.

1 The supremacy of Jesus

Hebrews 1

Hebrews plunges us straight in at the deep end. In these opening verses we find some of the richest theology of the New Testament. Nevertheless, these verses are also an introduction, in that they set out the key themes of the letter: the continuity with Judaism, yet the superiority of Jesus compared with what went before; Jesus' nature as superior to (and distinct from) angels or other spiritual beings; Jesus' unique perfection; Jesus' role as 'God in relation to the world'; and Jesus' priestly role in bringing complete purification for sins. All of these ideas will be explored in more detail.

The overriding point of this passage is that Jesus is greater than anything that has come before, and anything that could possibly come after. There is a real danger for Christianity that, in as much as it argues that Jesus fulfilled and renewed God's promises of old, sometimes in surprising ways, there might be nothing to stop the same happening again a few hundred years later—the 'new covenant' being replaced by an 'even newer covenant'. This is not merely a theoretical possibility; Islam effectively does make this claim. Islamic theology suggests that Jesus was indeed a great prophet—in many ways greater than those before him—but that he was 'replaced' by Muhammad, who provided the final, full revelation 600 years later. Hebrews tries to cut out this possibility in advance. There can be no possibility of anyone in the future surpassing Jesus, because Jesus is the 'heir of all things' (v. 2). He was the agent at work in creation (see Proverbs 8:22–31) and has been responsible for sustaining it ever since. He is the 'reflection of God's glory and the exact imprint of God's very being' (v. 3). It could be claimed that all humanity reflects God's glory, since we are made in God's image—hence the importance of 'the exact imprint of God's very being' ('imprint' is the word used of a mark in wax made by a stamp). The claim is designed to leave no 'wiggle room': Jesus is the perfect revelation of God (compare John 1:1–14; Colossians 1:15–20; Philippians 2:5–11).

The attempt to prove that Jesus is superior to the angels may seem odd to us. It provides a good reminder that, as we read, we are entering a different cultural world. Some of the language used here can appear to suggest that Jesus' high status was given to him only at some point in his life (for example, 'appointed', v. 2, and 'today', v. 5 quoting Psalm 2:7; compare Romans 1:4; Acts 13:33), but the reference to Jesus work in creation (v. 2) makes this impossible. Either these are simply poetic ways of describing God's eternal relationship with Jesus or they point to Jesus' status being publicly declared rather than changing (compare Philippians 2:9–11).

If you want to see or hear from God, look at and listen to Jesus; we can see God perfectly in the face of Jesus Christ. These are profound claims, which separate Christianity from other religions and spiritualities. Are we conscious of how profound they are?

2 Lower 'for a little while'

Hebrews 2:1–9

'Carrot and stick' is an accurate, if rather blunt, description of much of Hebrews. It contains very strong warnings against 'drifting away', coupled with warm encouragements. Here we begin with a warning. The unique exalted status of Jesus means that to ignore him would be a great crime—indeed, since he is the face of God, a great sin. This is an element of Christianity that we tend not to stress today, believing that 'fire and brimstone' preaching achieves nothing and that the message about Jesus should always be 'good news'. However, we should note that Hebrews' warnings not to drift away are addressed to those who are already 'insiders'; they have nothing to do with preaching to people outside the community.

The 'message declared through angels' (v. 2) refers to the Jewish belief at the time that the Law was given to Moses via angels (compare Galatians 3:19). Thus 'angels' in this passage sets up contrasts both between humans and angels (or spiritual powers) and between the message of Jesus and traditional Judaism.

Verses 5–9 provide a remarkable interpretation of Psalm 8. The psalm contains two ambiguities: first, are humans made 'a little lower' or 'lower for a little while', and, second, are they lower 'than God' or 'than the angels'? In respect to the first question, it is natural to read Psalm 8 as meaning 'a little lower' but now, in the light of Jesus, the writer sees a deeper, different meaning. The second question can be argued either way, but the Greek translation of Psalm 8 makes it refer unambiguously to angels. All together we have an apparent problem, for Psalm 8:4, with its mention of the 'son of man', was an obvious reference point for Jesus' use of 'Son of Man', but it appears to say, particularly in the Greek translation, that Jesus as Son of Man was 'lower' than the angels. This is a problem in particular since 'the angels' were responsible for the Jewish law, so this interpretation would undermine the idea that Jesus takes priority over the law.

In a master-stroke, Hebrews solves this problem and produces a significant piece of pastoral theology. The author reads the psalm as saying 'for a little while lower than the angels' (vv. 7, 9), referring to Jesus' humble life and suffering death (v. 9). Thus Jesus' superiority to the angels is preserved, except during his willing emptying of himself. Furthermore, this means that the 'Son of Man' underwent a period of suffering before exaltation (vv. 7–8; compare Philippians 2:5–11), which provides comfort for the readers of the letter who are also suffering. It will only be 'for a little while' and then they too will be exalted. Is that a comfort to us?

3 Jesus our brother

Hebrews 2:10–18

'It was fitting…' says the writer (v. 10). He is not arguing from the scriptures but from Jesus' life: he knows that Jesus suffered and died, and, on reflection, sees a divine plan within those circumstances. He says that Jesus 'had to' (v. 17) become human so that he could help humans (v. 18). He connects this obligation to Jesus' role as high priest—a priest being from among the people, acting on behalf of them all—and the need to destroy the power of death through death (v. 14). Throughout the New Testament,

Jesus' death is often said to have been 'necessary', but no further explanation is given: here the writer attempts one. Presumably the train of thought is that (a) the death happened; (b) it was so terrible that, if it happened, it must have been the only way salvation could have been achieved; and (c) perhaps we can grasp some reasons for it (for example, this argument about priesthood) but, even if we can't, (a) and (b) still stand.

The conclusion is that Jesus was, and is, truly our brother who was like us—was tested and suffered. But this is not just about the past; notice the word 'is' in verse 18. Jesus may now be exalted but he has taken his experience of suffering with him, so he remains able to sympathise and understand (see 4:14–16).

Referring to Jesus as our brother is not a common aspect of most Western Christianity, although Jesus as 'elder brother' is a key concept in much African Christology. It expresses a sense of closeness and 'alongside-ness', with the idea that he pioneers a path we can follow (v. 10). Similarly, the idea of a high priest offering sacrifices is alien to most of us. Within Judaism, however, the priests were 'normal people', farming and living in towns, going up to Jerusalem occasionally to do their temple service (Joshua 21:13–19; Luke 1:5–9). Thus there was a real sense that a priest 'understood' and was 'one of us'. Hebrews fastens on to this, insisting that despite the fact that Jesus is truly exalted and supreme, he is also close to us—one of us, who understands.

It's hard to hold these two aspects of Jesus together. Theologians have argued out creedal statements expressing this truth, but what matters more is its place in our lives. Many of us, in practice, see Jesus either as a model human whom we might try to imitate but who can't actually help us, or as an exalted god-figure, awesome and distant, able to help but too busy, great or holy to be concerned for us. No, says Hebrews, the 'exact imprint of God's very being' is also our brother who shares our flesh and blood, suffering and temptation. Do you see Jesus as your brother?

4 Do not harden your hearts

In chapters 3 and 4, Israel's exodus experience is used to provide a warning. Before this, though, the writer wants to make clear that Jesus is in continuity with, but also greater than, Moses (just as he was greater than the angels). He does this by bringing together Numbers 12:7, where God says, 'My servant Moses… is entrusted with/faithful in all my house', and 1 Chronicles 17:11–14, where God says to David, 'I will raise up your offspring after you… one of your sons… shall build a house for me… he shall be a son to me… I will confirm him [or, in the Greek translation of Chronicles, 'appoint him faithful'] in my house and in my kingdom for ever'. Thus the Old Testament itself used the same language of 'faithful in my house' to refer to both Moses, a servant, and a future figure, a son, who will actually be the builder of the house. Thus the Jewish scriptures point to 'one greater than Moses' coming—greater because a 'son' is greater than a 'servant', and the builder is greater than the house (and the servants within it). This last point seems strange, which is why we have verse 4: God creates everything and is clearly greater than his creation; thus the builder is greater than the house. The detail here is perhaps too much for many of us; nevertheless, we can appreciate that it was important for a scripture-focused Jewish audience that the scriptures themselves should support the claims being made about Jesus.

The quotation in verses 7–11 (partially repeated in verse 15, 4:3 and 4:7) is from Psalm 95:7–11, summarising the events in Numbers 13—14. This was the occasion when, quite shortly after the exodus and the giving of the law at Sinai, the Israelites sent spies into Canaan. The majority of the spies told the people that the land was occupied by giants and too strongly defended for them to enter; the people accepted this verdict, grumbled against God and decided to return to Egypt. Thus it depicts a moment when, after being rescued by God and hearing from God, the people lost heart and chose to go back in their lack of faith rather than forward, trusting God. This is a direct parallel to the position of the readers of Hebrews: they too have set off with God and need to 'hold our first confidence firm to the end' (v. 14). Are we in the same situation in some area of life?

5 Beginning is not enough

Hebrews 4:1–14

This passage continues the interpretation of Psalm 95, picking up the phrase, 'in my anger I swore, "They shall not enter my rest"'. The fact that these words occur in the psalm (attributed to David) reveals to the writer that this 'rest' cannot simply mean the entry into Canaan, which eventually Israel did achieve before David was even born, but must point forward to a future 'rest' (vv. 7–8). At least, it must have application as a prophecy for future times.

Thus the scriptures describe some who received the good news (that is, accepted it and began the journey of faith) but failed to enter the rest because of disobedience (v. 6). If this happened to many who experienced God's saving act in the exodus, presumably it could also happen to many who experienced God's saving act in Jesus. Beginning is not sufficient; we need to remain obedient/faithful and so 'enter the rest' (v. 11). God cannot be deceived (vv. 12 13): he knows the state of our hearts.

This is a frightening passage, for it puts a large 'If...' in front of our hopes. They are not certain, for while God may be dependable and trustworthy, we may not be. There is a conditionality about our future hope; it depends on us not falling into disobedience. It is not easy to hold together this assertion of conditionality with the truth that 'all has been accomplished' (for example, John 19:30; Hebrews 9:12, 24–26) and 'nobody can snatch you out of my hands' (John 10:28; Romans 8:31–39). Indeed, many theologians have wrestled with this seeming contradiction. Two observations might help. First, these different messages seem to be given in different contexts: when there is complacency, the conditionality is stressed; when there is fear and anxiety, the security is emphasised. Second, there is an obvious difference between saying that nobody else can snatch you out of God's hand and saying that you yourself might make future choices that will put you outside God's grace. Indeed, within the Old Testament, although the people were chosen as a nation by God's free grace, individuals could still put themselves outside the covenant (Numbers 15:30–31).

6 A merciful high priest

Hebrews 4:15—5:14

Thankfully, the emphasis now switches back to encouragement. The conditionality has not been dropped; there is still the need to 'hold fast to our confession' (4:14), and yet the emphasis here is on our confidence that we will receive help from God (v. 16). Thus, in these opening chapters of Hebrews we have switched back and forth, between carrot and stick. Hebrews 2:1–9 and then 3:1—4:14 warn us not to fall away; 2:10–18 and 4:15—5:10 encourage us that Jesus understands our weaknesses.

Chapter 4:14–16 looks back directly to 2:17–18, where Jesus is introduced as a 'high priest' who was tested himself and so can be a source of mercy, atonement and salvation for us. Those who are struggling and in danger of 'falling back' should be confident that God will not abandon them: if they turn to him, they will receive the grace they need to remain faithful.

This mention of 'high priest' sets up the discussion in 5:1–10 of Jesus' priesthood, culminating in the declaration that he is a 'high priest according to the order of Melchizedek' (v. 10). This assertion is repeated in 6:20, before being explored more fully in the following chapter. The reason for the Melchizedek link will be explored in the notes on chapter 7. For now, we observe the continuation of the theme of our solidarity with Jesus: a high priest is 'one of the people', working on their behalf (v. 1), who understands and sympathises with their weaknesses (v. 2), and is appointed by God (v. 4). There is a difference, for a human high priest needs to offer sacrifice for his own sins (v. 3), yet Jesus, despite his testing, did not sin (4:15). This, however, is not the focus here. Rather, we are given Jesus as both a help and an example. He is a help because his experience means that he deals gently with us (v. 2) and we know that he is heard by God (v. 7). He is an example because, although he was God's Son, he too needed to endure suffering, and only through this did he receive God's blessing (vv. 8–10). We can be encouraged that in our suffering we can get help, and that these sufferings in no way imply that we are not precious to God. (This idea is developed further in chapter 12.)

This week's readings seem to have been heady stuff, full of rich theology with great pastoral meaning. However, so far, apparently, we have just received milk, not solid food. Get ready for next week!

Guidelines

We are all under pressure. Our readings this week have spoken into this situation, emphasising that Jesus, the perfect representation of God, also suffered, and that now, as our brother and high priest, he can walk alongside us, understanding our weaknesses and bringing help in our trials. The example of his life shows that suffering is part of the life of the people of God, though it will not continue for ever. We must also play our part, continuing in obedience and trust.

Is there an area of your life in which you need to consciously invite Jesus as your brother to come and walk alongside you? Do you fall into despair, thinking that suffering will continue for ever, or that suffering proves you are not loved by God? Do you need to hear and respond to the exhortation to continue in obedience, recognising the possibility of drifting away? 'We must pay greater attention to what we have heard' (2:1): what is God saying to you?

1 Beyond God's reach?

Hebrews 6:1–12

Once again we find both encouragement and stern warning. The encouragement is warm: the readers are capable of far more than mere milk; they are not dull. Like Jesus, they are headed for perfection (v. 1; compare 5:9). The writer is confident in them (v. 9), calling to mind a particular expression of their love (v. 9–10), which should probably be seen as a reference to their faithfulness to God in a time of persecution and their support for those who were imprisoned (see 10:32–34).

Nevertheless, we have to face head-on the stern warning that 'it is impossible to restore again to repentance those who have once been enlightened… and then have fallen away' (vv. 4–6). This seems to imply that it is possible to be beyond the reach of the good news of Christ, which seems to contradict the thrust of the Christian message. This passage and the quite similar one at 10:26–31 have been the focus of much attention through

Christian history, both by those seeking to ameliorate their apparent starkness and by those advocating a harsh response to 'sinners' (indeed, these verses provided one of the reasons why the practice developed of delaying baptism until near death).

If we are right to say that nobody is beyond the reach of God's love, there are three possible ways of looking at this passage. First, we could say that the author is overstating his case out of a desire to impact his readers, though that seems rather like an attempt to water down passages that we find unpalatable. Second, the verbs that follow 'fallen away' in verse 6 ('are crucifying again... are holding him up') can be read as temporal ('while they are crucifying again...') rather than causal ('since they are crucifying...'), which would mean, effectively, 'they cannot be brought to repentance while they are still sinning'. This is something of a truism, however: of course you can't repent while you are still sinning. Third, we could focus on the word 'impossible' and quote Mark 10:27, where, in response to the disciples' exclamation 'Then who can be saved?', Jesus says, 'For mortals it is impossible, but not for God; for God all things are possible.' Thus, in effect, Hebrews would be saying, 'We cannot restore to repentance...'. Those who have fallen away cannot simply start acting differently and rejoin the community, but this does not preclude a new 'conversion' experience at the hands of God, who makes the dead alive and brings light out of darkness. How do you come to grips with this stern warning?

2 Abraham and Melchizedek

Hebrews 6:13—7:14

The first part of this passage (6:13–20) continues the sense of encouragement and confidence that followed the stern warning in 6:1–8. The link is the idea of those who 'through faith and patience inherit the promises' (v. 12). 'Faith', 'inherit' and 'promises', taken together, easily bring Abraham to mind, and Abraham then leads back to the figure of Melchizedek (v. 20), who has already been mentioned in 5:10 and will be properly explained in 7:1–22.

Two reasons for confidence, despite the stern warning, are presented, in addition to the one already given (6:9–12) about their faithfulness in the persecution. First, there is the fact that we are the heirs to the promise to Abraham (6:17; compare Galatians 3:6–29), and that promise, reinforced by God's oath, cannot fail (v. 18). Second, there is our solidarity with Jesus, who has pioneered our salvation (v. 20; compare 2:10), going before us into God's presence as our great high priest, giving us the confidence to approach God and receive mercy and grace (v. 19; compare 4:14–16).

Many people wonder why the author introduces Melchizedek. The reason seems to be that he is trying to respond to two potential challenges to the idea of Jesus as our high priest. First, according to Moses, Jesus could not be a priest because he was not descended from Aaron, but was of the tribe of Judah (7:13–14). Thus Hebrews needs to establish that the Jewish scriptures themselves point to there being another 'order' of priests. Second, the fact that the scriptures point to another priesthood can be taken as demonstrating that the existing, levitical priesthood was limited and temporary (7:11). Indeed, because Abraham treated Melchizedek as his superior (7:1–10), and Abraham is the father of Israel, Melchizedek has to be seen as superior to Israel and its law. Thus the one who is 'of the order of Melchizedek' (or whom Melchizedek resembles: 7:3) will be superior to the law.

This argument about Melchizedek has little significance for many of us, because the ideas about the Jewish priesthood mean little to us. We can focus, however, on the sense that God's word can be trusted. What happened in Jesus might seem new, but in fact it is in full accordance with the scriptures. Indeed, they point to it. God did not 'move the goalposts'; nor will he today.

3 The perfect priest

Hebrews 7:15–28

The fact that the scriptures point to another priesthood, and thus to the temporary nature of the levitical priesthood, is further developed. In Psalm 110:4 God proclaims someone 'a priest for ever according to the order of Melchizedek'. This priest will not die, as the levitical priests 'of the order of Aaron' do. The idea of an eternal priesthood was also hinted at when Melchizedek was introduced earlier (7:3: 'having neither beginning of days nor end of life' and 7:8: 'In the one case, tithes are received by those who are mortal; in the other, by one of whom it is testified that he lives').

So who qualifies as this 'priest for ever'? Well, Jesus does because of the 'power of an indestructible life' (v. 16). His resurrection proves that he is indeed the priest mentioned in the scriptures.

Furthermore, Jesus the ever-living priest is a better priest. This is explained in a number of different ways. The former system was 'weak and ineffectual' (v. 18)—in contrast, it seems, to the 'power' (v. 16) that was at work in Jesus, particularly at his resurrection. The 'eternal' priest is always there to save and intercede, unlike a constantly changing series of priests (vv. 23–25). Jesus himself was perfect—he didn't sin (4:15)—and therefore is better able to offer sacrifices because he does not need to atone for his own sins (vv. 26–28). Jesus' priesthood has been established by God's oath, which is more dependable than the words of the law mediated by angels (6:16–18). It is also mentioned that Jesus needs to offer sacrifices once only, as opposed to a continuing cycle of sacrifices (v. 27), that he is 'exalted above the heavens' (v. 26), that we can 'approach God through him' (v. 25) and that 'he offered himself' (v. 27). These ideas will be important in chapters 8—10.

Once again, the contrast between two systems of priesthood can seem somewhat arcane to us. Perhaps the focus for us is the sense that Jesus brings a 'better covenant' (v. 22), because regulations and laws are, in the end, weak and ineffectual, depending on transient, imperfect people. We too can try to pin our hopes on transient, imperfect institutions.

4 We have a high priest

'We have this kind of high priest' (v. 1)—that is, the kind that has been described earlier (holy and blameless, 7:26–28) and the kind that is about to be described (seated at God's right hand and ministering in the true sanctuary, 8:1–5).

This claim most probably had a double significance for the original readers. If they were Jews who found themselves estranged from traditional Judaism because of their loyalty to Jesus, it is quite likely that the lack of a physical priesthood was a cause of real anxiety. The temple in Jerusalem provided assurance that sin could be dealt with, which was of great significance to Jews, even those who were too far away ever to go there. Thus, the writer asserts, 'we have a high priest': in choosing Jesus, we are not losing the spiritual help that a high priest gives. Indeed, 'we have this kind of high priest', one who is superior in various ways to the one they have left behind. But this is not merely a theological exercise demonstrating Jesus' superiority to 'the Jewish law': the 'main point', that we do have a high priest, probably spoke to a deep pastoral need.

The superiority of the heavenly sanctuary in which Jesus makes his offering is further explored in chapter 9. Here, however, a key point of exegesis is presented, for the writer points us to Exodus 25:40, where Moses is instructed to build the 'tent' (shrine/tabernacle) according to the pattern shown him on the mountain (v. 5; see also Exodus 26:30; 27:8; Numbers 8:4). The word 'pattern' might easily be translated 'model', and Exodus and Numbers imply that Moses saw a vision of a sanctuary, which he was to copy. Thus the scriptures reveal that the sanctuary built by Moses was only a copy of a greater original. It was but a shadow of the true, heavenly sanctuary. Thus, not only do we have a better high priest, but he offers sacrifices in a sanctuary of which the temple in Jerusalem is only a pale imitation. Finally, using Jeremiah 31:31–34, the writer again asserts that the scriptures point to a new, better covenant marked by inner spirituality rather than external laws (v. 10).

The Hebrew believers should not be anxious about their loss of connection with the physical high priest and temple, for in their place they have a greater high priest and a temple of which the physical one was a mere copy. They have not left the covenant but have exchanged the obsolete one for a new, spiritual covenant. It is worth examining what we think we have lost because of our choice of Christ, to see whether in some way what was lost has been replaced.

5 Approaching God

Hebrews 9:1–14

This passage falls into two parts. First (vv. 1–10), the writer uses the design of the tent built by Moses to make a spiritual point. It was not really a single tent, but two—the first or front one, which was in general use, and the second, rear, most holy one, to which access was extremely restricted (v. 7). The meaning that the writer has found in this (by God's inspiration, v. 8) is that the first tent actually keeps people out of the second. Opening up free access to the second, most holy tent would require removing the first tent. So, too, if access into God's presence through Jesus is to be achieved (see 4:14; 10:19–20), the front tent, the first tent, needs to be swept away. What was designed as part of the system of access to God in fact functioned as, or at least represents, a blockage.

Second (vv. 11–14), the writer summarises the priestly work of Christ, which he will examine further in the following chapter. This sacrifice was offered in a greater temple/tent, once only, and was of his own blood. Its effect is to cleanse the inner spirit, the conscience, not just the external flesh.

That Christ offered himself as a sacrifice (v. 12) has been mentioned in passing earlier (7:27). It represents a startling theological move, for the priest and the sacrifice are normally distinct. The priest sacrifices the animal but does not sacrifice anything in the modern sense of 'willingly giving up something precious'. Here, however, Jesus is both priest and sacrifice; his action is complete in itself.

Many Jews in Jesus' day had started to question the purpose of the sacrifices offered in the temple, for they too could see that the blood of animals could not actually purify the conscience (vv. 13–14): externals do not change one's inner spiritual state. The Jewish philosopher Philo tells us that many saw the value as being in obedience: offering the sacrifices mattered, not because the blood of goats intrinsically does something but because, by offering them, worshippers were being obedient to what God had commanded. Also around this time (though the date is hard to fix), particular significance was being given to the 'binding of Isaac' (Genesis 22), interpreted as a story of Isaac willingly embracing death. Thus the logic that a willing self-sacrifice has spiritual value of a different order to animal sacrifices would have made sense to the original readers. Although animal sacrifices are alien to us, it is worth reflecting on whether we think there is spiritual value in actions of themselves (going to church, giving to the poor and so on) or whether the value lies in our intentions and motives.

6 The supreme offering

Hebrews 9:15–28

Why did Jesus need to die? Couldn't salvation have been achieved in a different way? Rarely does the New Testament try to answer these questions. Instead it takes as facts both Jesus' death and that this was part of the plan for salvation, and concludes simply that it was 'necessary' (see, for example, Mark 8:31). Hebrews, though, tries to provide an explanation. The author argues (vv. 16–17) that, in normal life, a will becomes effective only upon the death of the one who makes it. Thus it is necessary to have a death for a will to become effective. But the Greek word for a 'will' is the same as the word for a 'covenant'. Thus, it is necessary to have a death for a covenant to become effective. This is confirmed by the account of the inauguration of the 'first covenant' by Moses (vv. 18–21; Exodus 24:1–8). Thus, to bring in a new covenant, to provide forgiveness, a death was also necessary (v. 22).

The same argument also has force in reverse. The fact that the death occurred is further demonstration that Jesus was inaugurating a new covenant (v. 15). We probably have to admit that this attempt to explain why Jesus needed to die falls flat for us, who speak a language in which 'will' and 'covenant' are distinct, and who do not share the cultural and religious assumption that 'without the shedding of blood there is no forgiveness' (v. 22). Perhaps we should simply read this as a demonstration of the importance of working hard to express and explain the gospel message within any given language and culture.

Verses 23–25 recap on earlier ideas about the superiority of the heavenly sanctuary and that Jesus was both priest and sacrifice (see 9:11–14). Then (vv. 25–26) the writer develops further the idea that this sacrifice happened once only (mentioned in 9:12). This point emerges from the idea that Jesus was both priest and sacrifice. A priest can repeat an animal sacrifice time and time again, with fresh animals. However, sacrificing oneself, offering one's own blood, can only happen once, because a person can only die once. Thus, indeed, Jesus has now 'sat down at the right hand of the Majesty on high' (1:3, alluded to in 8:1) because his sacrifice can only, and need only, happen once. Interestingly, Psalm 110, which contains the reference to an eternal priest of the order of Melchizedek, also refers to 'my lord' sitting down at God's right hand (v. 1). Jesus' work is final and complete. When he returns, he will not need to deal with sin (v. 28). This truth that the work of Christ is already complete, that all was accomplished at Jesus' death, can bring us great freedom and security.

Guidelines

'All my hope on God is founded' declares a popular hymn. But is it? In our readings this week, we have seen the original readers challenged over the value they gave to the visible institutions of temple and priesthood, to regulations and laws, and to the familiar structures of their lives and religious practices. They were encouraged to look beyond these structures to God himself, who is trustworthy and has provided and completed all that is needed. It takes some imagination to grasp the mindset and cultural world of the original readers. What would be the equivalent for us today of the security of priest, temple and the sacrificial system? How deeply and securely do you believe that Christ's work is complete, that nothing more need be done except to continue in faith and obedience? What different does, or could, that make in your life?

1 Doing God's will

Hebrews 10:1–18

This passage recaps the previous two chapters' description of the new covenant brought in by Jesus' high-priestly work of offering himself in the heavenly temple. In doing so, the writer brings together three biblical passages. First (vv. 5–7) comes a new passage, Psalm 40:6–8. This describes someone written of in the scriptures, for whom God prepares a body and who 'comes' to do God's will in contrast to the sacrifices and offerings laid down in the law. Unsurprisingly, the writer sees here a prophecy of Jesus' incarnation (v. 5). This is relevant in two ways: it is another example of the scriptures themselves pointing to the temporary, limited nature of the sacrificial system, and it establishes 'doing God's will', obedience, as the key spiritual activity. This accords with the way Jesus has been described in Hebrews 5:7–8 and, indeed, with Jesus' own teaching (for example, Mark 3:35; Matthew 21:28–32). It also fits within emerging Jewish theology (see notes on Hebrews 9:1–14).

Then, in verse 12, we have an allusion to Psalm 110:1. The idea of Jesus 'sitting down' appears three times at key moments in Hebrews (1:3; 8:1; 12:2), and is important in the argument that his sacrifice is made but once (vv. 11–12, noting that the priests 'stand' day after day, since their work is never complete). Psalm 110:4 has also been crucial, for this is the verse about 'a priest for ever according to the order of Melchizedek'. The second part of Psalm 110:1, 'until I make your enemies your footstool' (quoted earlier at Hebrews 1:13), is important elsewhere as a declaration of Jesus' Lordship and also as an explanation of his current absence (for example, Matthew 22:41–44; Acts 2:33–35; 3:20–21). It is similar to Psalm 8:6, quoted at Hebrews 2:8 and picked up, for example, in 1 Corinthians 15:27.

Finally we have an extract from Jeremiah 31:33–34 (quoted in full at Hebrews 8:8–12). Not only does this speak of a new covenant (implying the obsolescence of the old: 8:13) of the spirit and heart, not of regulations, but it also says that God will no longer remember sin—in which case there need be no more sacrifices (v. 18). Thus Jeremiah supports the idea that Jesus' one sacrifice, 'offered for all time' (v. 12), brings the endless round of sacrifices to an end.

It is valuable to reflect on our own church practices and spiritual lives: what matters is 'doing God's will'.

2   Therefore...

Hebrews 10:19–39

Now we come to the turning point in Hebrews, when, with the word 'Therefore...' (v. 19), the writer moves from his theological exposition to urge its practical outworkings. Of course, we have already had stern warnings about falling back (for example, 3:12; 4:1; 6:4–8) and encouragement to 'hold firm' and 'go forward' (3:6; 4:11, 16; 6:1). Nevertheless, this point fills out more systematically the warnings and encouragements that have peppered the previous chapters.

Three things are urged of us—that we approach God with confidence because of what Jesus has done (gone 'through the curtain', that is, into the holy of holies, 6:19; 9:1–10), that we hold on to confession without wavering, and that we provoke one another to love and good deeds (which includes the need to meet together). The fact that the possibility of this confident approach to God has been the focus of the theological argument of the letter suggests that the point is foundational. It is this access to God, with its dimensions of forgiveness, a new covenant and a great high priest, that provides the motivation and security necessary to hold to the confession and act with love.

Verses 32–39 describe 'those earlier days' in which the community underwent persecution. At this time there was great pressure not to hold fast to the confession, and to withdraw from visible association with other believers, but they withstood those pressures. Nevertheless, we get the feeling that the writer is anxious that this situation will not continue. Thus, perhaps, we see the logic of Hebrews: the writer is worried that the believers will fall away from the confession of faith and love for each other, so he has written this letter, which, in part, contains warnings and exhortations but fundamentally seeks to give the people confidence in approaching God. He also, here, calls to mind the example of their praiseworthy actions in the past and, in chapter 11, will give many more examples. The point that Jesus will not delay (v. 37) connects with the interpretation of Psalm 110:1 earlier (10:12–13; also 9:28).

Verses 26–31 are very similar to 6:4–8 (which was also followed by a reference to the believers' action in 'serving the saints': 6:10; similar to 10:34). We will not look again at the detail here, except to note that it starts, 'If we wilfully persist in sin…' (v. 26), which perhaps suggests that both passages refer to the impossibility of forgiveness and access to God while one is, in words or actions, denying Christ.

Nevertheless, we should hear again the exhortation to approach God with confidence because of what Jesus has done, hold on to our faith without wavering and provoke one another to love and good deeds.

3 Faith

Faith is not 'believing in things which are not true', but in things which are not yet visible. The Christian activist Jim Wallis describes Christian hope as 'believing in spite of the evidence and watching the evidence change'. Thus verse 1: 'Faith is the assurance of things hoped for'—that is, faith is trusting in things that will happen, but have not yet happened. This belief is, in fact, deeply in tune with the nature of the universe, for the whole universe once did not exist, was not seen, but then it was brought into being and became visible (v. 3). Before anything 'is', there has to be a stage when it is 'not yet'.

Hebrews presents us with a glorious list of heroes from the Bible (and, in verses 34–38, from more recent Jewish history). It is a long list—though, given that we are only up to Genesis 22 by verse 19, it could have been much longer! It is worth reading in one go, however, to get the sense of the long, almost endless story of the faithful people of God, all of whom had been in the same position as the readers are—needing to hold fast and press on despite the fact that the promised outcome was not yet visible.

This is a message of timeless application, but it was perhaps particularly necessary for the original readers. They felt that they had left traditional Judaism, with its visible temple and sacrificial system, and were having to rely on the invisible (remember 8:1: 'the main point… is this: we have such a high priest'). Indeed, they were also waiting for Jesus' return (9:28; 10:25), which had not yet happened. Thus the writer reminds them that the story of God's people, the true story of Judaism, had always been a story of faith in what was not visible, trust in what had not yet happened. What they were experiencing was not a sign that their beliefs were defective, but rather a sign that they were fully in line with the revelation of God in the past.

There is a final theological twist, however, in verse 40, for here we find that we are not actually following these past heroes. Rather, they have been waiting to benefit from the work of Christ ('perfection', v. 40; see 10:14; 5:9). Heroes such as Abraham and Moses receive what was promised only because of the work of Christ.

4 Suffering

Hebrews 12:1–13

Here we find the basic exhortation from 10:26–39 repeated in the light of chapter 11 and using the common metaphor of life as a race (found in contemporary Greek writers as well as in Paul: for example, 1 Corinthians 9:24; Philippians 3:12–14). This works well as a metaphor, for it allows the writer to depict the journey that Jesus took, from his earthly life, through suffering and death, to his place at God's right hand, and assures us that, with Jesus as our pioneer (2:10), we too can follow the same route. This will involve suffering 'for a little while' (2:9; 5:8), as it did for him, but the destination is to go 'through the curtain' as Jesus did (10:20; see 6:19) to the throne of God (or, as 12:22 puts it, to the city of the living God). There are parallels with Jesus' exhortation to 'take up your cross and follow me' (Mark 8:34).

The question of suffering needs more consideration. Their suffering seems to have been making the readers doubt that they were part of God's people. They were 'losing heart' as they succumbed to the near-universal temptation to assume that if we are suffering, we must have displeased God. The writer has two responses. First, he points them to the example of Jesus, God's Son, who was exalted to God's right hand (so he did not displease God) yet had to endure the cross (v. 2). Second, he quotes Proverbs 3:11–12 (vv. 5–6). By his interpretation, this passage does not just disprove the notion that their suffering means God is not with them; rather, being disciplined by God shows that they are his true children, rather than illegitimate ones (12:8). Suffering can actually prove that we are among God's children.

Suffering remains a terrible curse in this world and the question 'Why does God allow suffering?' is an intractable problem. This passage does not provide an 'answer' to it, just as neither Job nor Jesus received an answer from God. However, it does decisively reject the all-too-common belief (particularly in the secret place of our own hearts) that, if we are suffering, it is because we 'deserve it'. It would be foolish and pastorally wicked to twist the passage into saying that all suffering is 'God's discipline' and is in some way 'good for you'. Nevertheless, right at the heart of Christianity is the fact that Jesus' suffering produced great good. These are difficult issues:

what is most important, with this passage, is to reject the devil's lie that 'if you were the child of God, you would not suffer' (see Matthew 4:3–4).

5 Pursuing peace and holiness

Hebrews 12:14–29

The metaphor of the race continues as we are exhorted to pursue peace and holiness (v. 14). Then we have three allusions to the Old Testament. The first is to the 'root of bitterness', a person 'whose heart is already turning away from the Lord our God' (Deuteronomy 29:18). This bitterness arises, perhaps, because of suffering, because the promise remains unseen. The emphasis in both Deuteronomy and Hebrews is on someone 'defiling' the broader community. With the phrase 'See to it that no one...' (vv. 15, 16) we seem to be in the world of a community looking after its members.

The second reference is to Esau, who, in Jewish thought, had become an archetype of an immoral person (vv. 16–17). The point, presumably, is that Esau sold his 'birthright', his place in his family, to gain a temporary respite from physical difficulty (hunger). This is parallel to the believers' temptation to gain respite in their sufferings by renouncing their place in God's family. The fact that 'later, when he wanted to inherit the blessing, he was rejected, for he found no chance to repent, even though he sought the blessing with tears', further illuminates the terrible passages in 6:4–8 and 10:26–31 about the impossibility of returning. In Esau's case, when he did later regret his actions and come seeking the blessing (Genesis 27:30–40), it simply wasn't possible for him to receive it; the opportunity had passed.

The third allusion is to Mount Sinai (vv. 18–21; see Deuteronomy 4:10–14). In an argument similar to the one used by Paul in Galatians 4:21–31, the writer accepts that the community is no longer 'at Sinai'—is no longer following the law given at a physical place, in fire, darkness, gloom and tempest. But this should not be seen as a deficit. On the contrary (vv. 22–24), they have come to the heavenly Jerusalem, the city of the living God, to a great heavenly festival, confident in the work of Jesus. It's the same idea as the one we saw in chapters 8—9: the lack of connection with the physical temple and human high priest is no loss, for instead they have a heavenly, better temple of which the physical is a mere copy, and a sinless, perfect high priest who offers his own life for them.

Again, though, this encouragement is accompanied by warning, this time picking up the thought of 2:1–3. The fact that they have direct access to God only makes it more serious if they reject his words. Letting a bitter root grow; swapping our place in God's family for physical respite or pleasure; failing to recognise or refusing to listen to God: perhaps one of these is something we need to consider more today.

6 Living it out

Hebrews 13

The letter comes to a close with a flurry of more general exhortations. It is as if the writer's planned exposition has come to an end—fittingly, with the arrival at the heavenly Jerusalem (12:22), the city of God, who is a consuming fire (12:29). Nevertheless, there are two themes within these exhortations—the fact that the Christians are marginal to, and excluded by, the wider community, and the relationship with leaders.

The suffering of the Christians at the hands of the wider community was discussed in 10:32–34. Now we have an even darker reference to those being tortured (v. 3). They are probably not people within this community (as implied by 12:4 and by the fact that this kind of persecution has not been mentioned earlier); nevertheless, the Christian community is under great threat. Verses 10–14 develop the theme further by overlaying two images—the burning of the holy animals outside the city, and Jesus himself dying outside the city. Thus, being outside or excluded from the wider community is, in fact, a place of holiness in imitation of Christ. In any case, they are destined now not for an earthly city, with an earthly temple, but a heavenly one (compare Philippians 3:20). Thus they should bear their sufferings without losing heart (12:3).

The sudden but emphatic mention of respect and obedience to leaders (vv. 7, 17–18) is intriguing, particularly the assertion that 'we' have been acting with a clean conscience. Perhaps the command is just a natural element of this kind of community exhortation. Perhaps it is particularly relevant for a community under pressure, which can easily become divided. It is possible, but not completely clear, that those mentioned in verse 7 were former leaders, perhaps the original missionaries (2:3). This is suggested by the past tense of 'spoke the word of God to you', the reference to the 'outcome' of their life and the declaration that Jesus remains the same (necessary if the example being cited is from the past). Of course, it could be that these are leaders absent because they are in prison (Timothy certainly has been: v. 23). The same could be said for the writer himself (v. 18), who hopes by their prayers to be restored to the fellowship.

The final blessing picks up the key element from the letter that the community's peace with God comes through the new, eternal covenant brought about through Jesus' sacrificial death ('blood' implying not just death but the offering of the blood on the altar: see 9:14). It also urges 'doing God's will', reminding us of the importance that has been placed on obedience to God (2:1; 5:7; 12:25) as opposed to carrying out the (ritual) practices laid down in the covenant from Moses (10:8–10). The writer characterises his work as a word of exhortation (v. 22), a good reminder that the point of theology is to affect the way we live.

Guidelines

We are urged to do God's will, to hold on to our faith without wavering, and to provoke each other to love and good deeds. This involves pressing on, even if the hoped-for outcome is not visible, even through suffering. Where is this perseverance particularly difficult for you at this time? In what areas of life is there a nagging temptation just to give up, to swap it all for an easier life? Let us approach God with confidence because of what Jesus, our priest and brother, has done for us, and seek God's grace and mercy in our difficulties, recognising that we do need to do our part and preserve our faith.

Success

We all want to be successful, including in our Christian faith, but what exactly should such success look like? Often, success is understood in terms of possession and achievement: the successful businesswoman buys a Rolls Royce and huge house, the successful athlete breaks world records, the successful entrepreneur builds a company from nothing to global domination and so on. But is success really about possession and achievement: are we successful only if we do more and get more? In particular, how does success play out in the life of a typical Christian? These short studies should help us to think a bit more about God's perspective on what constitutes a successful Christian life and ministry.

Quotations are taken from the New International Version of the Bible.

4–10 April

1 A successful prophet?

Jeremiah 38:1–13

You'd think that being a faithful man of God is a sure-fire route to success. This is certainly the case, provided we understand exactly what does, and what does not, constitute success. The ministry of the prophet Jeremiah is an excellent case study. He is faithful to his calling as a prophet, but that doesn't translate into physical comfort or material benefit—quite the opposite, in fact. As we read about his experiences as a prophet, it doesn't look as if Jeremiah had any visible success. When he dictates his prophecies to the scribe Baruch, some of the royal officials read them and respond with penitence, but King Jehoiakim shows nothing but contempt, burning the scroll a bit at a time as it is read to him (Jeremiah 36).

In today's reading, Jeremiah's preaching gets an extremely negative reaction: the royal officials are convinced that the only possible response is to kill him (v. 4). King Zedekiah's ambivalence is interesting: he doesn't oppose the plot to be rid of Jeremiah (v. 5) but later orders his rescue (vv. 7–10). Perhaps Jeremiah had a limited impact, even if he was unable to persuade the king of the truth of his message: this suggestion is borne out by the way chapter 38 develops, with the secret conversation between King Zedekiah and Jeremiah (vv. 14–27).

So although Jeremiah does have some impact, it comes at a price, and his ministry is not what the world would call a roaring success. He doesn't achieve his main aim of persuading the people to repent and return to the Lord, and his limited influence comes at the great price of sacrificing popularity and of personal risk to his life. But the vantage point of history makes it clear to us that Jeremiah was a successful prophet, provided we understand 'successful' as 'faithful'. Jeremiah faithfully proclaimed God's word to a generation that, in the main, didn't want to hear it. This was obviously frustrating for Jeremiah at times, and he complained to God on more than one occasion (see 12:1–4; 20:7–18), but the frustration never boiled over into a desertion of his calling. He remained faithfully steadfast, speaking the truth in love and refusing to be dissuaded from it, regardless of the opposition. His was a type of success that we would all do well to imitate.

2 The power of the healer?

Luke 17:11–19

Why are people sometimes so bad at expressing gratitude? This incident should give us pause for thought. Often we think that Jesus' ministry was always powerful and effective, and that healing automatically led to a living faith. If we read the Bible carefully, however, we discover a number of incidents like this one, where that does not seem to be the case.

Advocates of 'power evangelism' rightly point out the power of healing and miracles as a testimony to the love of God and the breaking in of the kingdom of God here on earth: 'tomorrow's bread today', as the saying goes. Yet not everyone responds to that bread in the way we might expect. The ten lepers all take the bread, as it were, and yet only one of them says 'thank you' and seeks a relationship with the giver. We cannot tell for certain if the other nine sought Jesus out later or never bothered, but Luke seems to be implying that it was only the Samaritan—whom Jews would have expected to be irreligious and uninterested in Jesus—who demonstrated living faith.

This relatively poor return (only one in ten who were healed showing any signs of faith) should not discourage us from praying for healing for all people, Christian and non-Christian alike, but it should warn us that divine healing does not necessarily lead to faith in Christ. We might equally reflect on the fact that many of those who were miraculously fed by Jesus came back to him primarily to get more food, and not because they understood the significance of what he had done for them (see John 6:25–40).

Jesus is concerned that the nine lepers did not respond in faith, but he also celebrates the one who did. This may be the lesson for us. We cannot expect automatic success in our ministry. Indeed, people may never express any thanks to us for it, even when it has greatly impacted them. The fact that God works in power in someone's life does not necessarily mean that the person will respond with a living faith, but we must celebrate when they do, and continue to pray and hope when they do not.

3 A painful calling

Ezekiel 24:15–27

Of all the Old Testament prophets, Ezekiel had one of the most painful callings, and the most agonising part of it comes in today's passage, when God takes his wife from him and orders him not to mourn. All of this was a sign to the people in exile for the way they would respond to the destruction of Jerusalem. The people's misplaced confidence in the temple and its institutions would be exposed as God took away the temple and all that it represented.

It is impossible for us to imagine the depths of agony that Ezekiel experienced. Knowing that his wife will die, he does not even spend his final day with her. Instead he spends time speaking with the people (v. 18). In the evening she dies, and Ezekiel carries on as if nothing had happened. It was not unusual for priests to be commanded not to mourn, in order to avoid ritual defilement (see Leviticus 21:1–4, 11–12), and yet the people want to know how his behaviour affects them (v. 19). They can see Ezekiel's unexpressed pain, and know by now that even in this there is probably a message for them.

Indeed there is. Just as Ezekiel was not observing the normal mourning customs, neither would the people mourn the destruction of the Jerusalem temple—not because of an absence of grief, but because the destruction would be so totally overwhelming. Even in the midst of such destruction and pain, however, it would be clear that God is sovereign (v. 24).

Ezekiel's experience indicates an important truth of the Christian life: choosing to obey God often leads directly to suffering. Ezekiel is successful as a prophet precisely because he does not mourn when his wife dies. In this way, he fulfils his calling to teach the people of Israel how they are to respond to the destruction of Jerusalem. Ezekiel's calling was a particularly hard one and God does not ask all of his servants to suffer quite so much, but successful Christian ministry is often anything but glamorous. Far from leading to achievement or acquisition of goods, it can have precisely the opposite result—a giving up of property or status. I can think of a faithful pastor in Japan, preparing to leaflet 12,000 homes on his own. As far as I know, he didn't get one response. Equally, an 84-year-old woman has devoted her whole life to caring for her brother, who has special needs. Both have suffered, but in different ways. It is only to be expected that we too will suffer, given that our pattern is Christ crucified.

4 Unafraid to question

Job 19

Job is a challenge to those who think that anyone who follows God will have an easy life. His experience exemplifies Jesus' warning that much will be required of those who have been given much (Luke 12:48). Job is greatly blessed with material possessions as well as a loving family, all of which fuels his heartfelt devotion to God (Job 1:1–5). But Job's greatest success is in the fact that he will not let his terrible loss get in the way of his relationship with God. He is relentless in pursuing the truth.

In today's passage, Job is clear about his devastation but also about his trust. He first expresses his pain. His supposed friends are becoming nothing but a crushing weight (vv. 2–3). He feels cut off from and oppressed by God (vv. 5–12), and isolated from society (vv. 13–19). This last point is of great significance in a society where individual identity is defined in terms of personal relationships. When he was a man of wealth and influence, others were eager to be with him; now that he has nothing, even the youngest and most insignificant in society abuse him (v. 18). Job has nothing and no one to turn to; he is reduced to skin and bone as he starves to death (v. 20).

Yet Job is still able to see beyond himself: he wants his words recorded, presumably so that others can learn from his experiences (vv. 23–24), and he is sure that his suffering will not be the end, that one day he will encounter God face to face (v. 25). This, then, is a sign of Job's success: an honest, open relationship with God that is primarily about God and not about Job.

At times, this relationship comes under immense strain. As the conversation with his friends continues, Job's frustration mounts, and sometimes his questioning strays beyond what is acceptable: he makes accusations that God does not answer (see 27:2; note also God's rebukes in Job 40—41). Yet he remains honest in his relationship with God, and, after expressing repentance (42:1–6), is commended by God (42:7).

Openness is at the heart of any successful relationship. We cannot always understand God's ways, as Job himself recognises, but we can be honest before God, and we can make God the centre of our relationships. Often, those who suffer can succeed in holding on to their faith only by being completely real about the way they feel. In the midst of the uncertainties and challenges of life, we can learn from Job's example of unfailing trust and uncompromising honesty.

5 Who knows what happened?

Acts 8:26–40

The story of Philip's meeting with the Ethiopian eunuch is a good reminder of the fact that we don't always get to see the 'successful outcome' of our efforts. This is true in many aspects of life, not least in Christian ministry. While we may wish we received such clear divine guidance (vv. 26, 29), we are quite likely to share at least one part of Philip's experience: he has no real idea of its long-term impact.

Philip is a model of faithful obedience. He goes where he is sent, speaks to those he meets, and moves on when it is time to do so. We, too, may sometimes meet people at very significant moments in their spiritual walk.

I have recently been involved with Christian Union missions to the three universities in Liverpool. It has been a week of many chance encounters. In one, two girls who hadn't been to church since coming to university decided they would start attending again. In another, an atheist philosophy student agreed to hear more about what it means to have faith in Jesus. Others were happy to talk, but a one-off encounter was quite sufficient for them. In each case, seeds were sown, but the truth is that we often don't know how successful we've been in these circumstances. Just as in the parable of the sower (Mark 4:1–20), we must liberally scatter the seed of the good news of the kingdom of God, knowing that not every seed will produce a crop.

Philip wasn't concerned with his achievements or his own gains from ministry, but with simple obedience to God's call. We should use the same criterion to determine how successful we are: remaining faithful and obedient is more important than any outward sign of success. Maybe one reason why Philip received the opportunity to minister to the Ethiopian was that he had absolutely no agenda of his own. If we trust that God is sovereign and that he is drawing people to himself, we can be content with simply initiating conversations about Jesus, or with helping someone to commit to Jesus but letting another Christian disciple them, or with working behind the scenes while others do more noticeable work. In these encounters, we are links in a chain: we do not have to do everything ourselves. Whatever part we have to play in another person's journey of faith, Philip's experience reminds us that it is God, by his Spirit, who draws people to himself; our success lies in obeying our calling and playing the part he gives us.

6 Suffering brings eternal glory

2 Corinthians 11:16–29

This short section brings together clearly both the agonies and the joys of Paul's lifelong service of Jesus. In his attempt to defend his own calling and ministry, Paul faces a difficult problem. He is trying to challenge a culture that focuses on individual achievements and abilities, so he doesn't really want to draw attention to what he himself has done. If he does, he will undermine the central point he is trying to make—that relationship with Christ is of much greater importance that anything we can do.

In effect, Paul is arguing against the world's definition of success, which we saw at the start of these studies, countering the idea that success means achievement and acquisition. So he makes it clear that boasting about one's own achievements is a supremely foolish thing to do. Adopting a slightly sarcastic tone, he agrees to play the world at its own game by boasting—but the difference is what he chooses to boast about. Thus Paul begins by making his pedigree clear (v. 22). He then develops his argument by listing his 'achievements'—the number of times he has been beaten, stoned, shipwrecked, mugged, hungry, thirsty, cold, stressed and troubled by other people (vv. 23–29).

Have you ever heard anyone else talk in this way? There is a certain machismo that boasts in endurance (number of miles run/weights lifted/hours worked and so on), but Paul's experience is both qualitatively and quantitatively different from our daily experience. He takes the most pride in his sufferings. It is natural to want to focus on the good things we have achieved in ministry, and Christianity in no way condones or promotes a masochistic view of life, but that doesn't mean we should ignore the challenge of Paul's experience and his dedication to Jesus, regardless of personal cost.

Paul's ministry was successful precisely because of the amount of anguish and pain that he experienced. He cared deeply for the people in his charge, so he suffered for them; he cared deeply for those who had never accepted Jesus, and was prepared to endure much so that they might have a chance to respond. If we want to see ourselves and others grow in faith, we will be engaging in a difficult war against the world, the flesh and the devil. Of course, we don't do anything in our own strength, but in the power of the Spirit. Nevertheless, while we should not deliberately seek pain or suffering, we must recognise that successful ministry will never be easy: we must be prepared for the cost. As Luther is reputed to have said, 'If Christ wore a crown of thorns, why do his followers expect to wear a crown of roses?'

Guidelines

The cross of Jesus is the obvious paradigm for thinking about a Christian understanding of success—so obvious that I have deliberately omitted it until now. Jesus was ultimately successful in his apparent failure: by dying, rejected and alone, he dealt with sin and won for us eternal life. We know this and love and worship him in response; but how deeply have we taken on board Paul's suggestion that we should imitate Christ's actions (Philippians 2:1–11)? This week's studies give us some concrete points to ponder further:

- Do we only equate 'success' with dramatic results? How does the story of the ten lepers speak to this?
- Are we happy to see success primarily in terms of faithfulness, regardless of the personal cost? How do the lives of Jeremiah, Ezekiel and Paul support this view?
- How successful are we at having an honest and open relationship with God, at involving him in the negative parts of our lives, and at accepting his silence but continuing to trust?
- How easily do we leave the outcomes of our endeavours to God? Are we happy simply to have chance encounters and trust that, in the proper time, God will reap an appropriate harvest?
- Do we believe that success is primarily about what we achieve and what we acquire, or are we prepared to leave all of that in God's hands?
- What, in your current situation, would God describe as a 'success'? Spend some time in prayer, asking him to tell you.

Finding peace of mind

Many people in our stressed and busy world, which is so full of choices to be made every day, find peace of mind an elusive quality. The Bible, too, is one long story of the search for peace with God and with one another. From beginning to end of the Old Testament, there is anguish stemming from rebellion against God, conflict between people, the experience of exile and continued oppression; and the New Testament letters are written, it seems, mainly to address a variety of disputes within the fledgling churches.

Yet peace is one of the greatest gifts that Jesus promised to his disciples: 'My peace I give you. I do not give to you as the world gives. Do not let your hearts be troubled and do not be afraid' (John 14:27). This peace, we note, is not 'as the world gives'. It does not depend on material security, strong locks and bolts and a settled future. It is peace despite, or in the middle of, uncertainty and potential loss: in the context of John 14, it is promised as the disciples face the imminent cataclysm in which the shepherd will be struck and the sheep will be scattered (see Mark 14:27).

The following six studies will explore just a few of the many facets of the peace of God—the ways in which it may be lost, found and maintained in our everyday lives and ministries. There will be practical advice from the Psalms, the teaching of Jesus and the apostles' letters, as well as things to be learnt from the words and lived experience of Old Testament prophets.

Quotations, unless otherwise stated, are taken from Today's New International Version of the Bible.

1 Freedom from condemnation

Romans 8:1–17

Paul makes a clear distinction in this passage between the mind focused on the 'desires' of the sinful nature and the mind fixed on what the Spirit 'desires' (vv. 5–6). The desires of the sinful nature, claims Paul, lead to 'death': a sense of condemnation before God, a recognition that we are slaves to our desires and our fears. The mind controlled by the sinful nature, then, is anything but peaceful. To experience 'life and peace', the mind needs to be controlled by the Holy Spirit—free from condemnation and secure in the knowledge that we are children who stand to inherit God's kingdom, not driven like slaves to obey a demanding master. This peace defies even physical death (v. 10): as Paul says elsewhere, 'Though outwardly we are wasting away, yet inwardly we are being renewed day by day' (2 Corinthians 4:16). So the peace that comes from the Spirit can override the anxieties associated with the physical decline and decay to which our bodies are subject.

What do the desires of the sinful nature feel like? James also attributes a lack of peace ('fights and quarrels') to the 'desires that battle within us' (James 4:1), and suggests that they stem from covetousness (v. 2) and the pursuit of pleasure above all (v. 3). So the sinful nature desires to acquire more and more, whether of material goods or physical comforts or power over other people. These are the desires that, if indulged, lead us to feel that we are struggling under a heavy weight, always looking over our shoulders to see what others have acquired, driven by discontentment, rather than enjoying the freedom and abundant life of the Spirit (see 2 Corinthians 3:17; John 10:10).

The peaceful mind is free of condemnation (v. 1) but this is, of course, different from the awareness of sin that leads to confession and forgiveness, which the Holy Spirit stirs up in us. Paul calls this 'godly sorrow... that leads to salvation and leaves no regret' (2 Corinthians 7:10). We might sometimes pray the final verse of Psalm 139: 'Search me, God and know my heart... See if there is any offensive way in me, and lead me in the way everlasting' (vv. 23–24). So those whose minds are led by the Spirit will be made aware of sin but not condemned by a burden of guilt; they will remain confident to approach God for forgiveness and peace.

2 Dwelling in God

Psalm 84

The Psalms are packed full of the search for peace amid various sources of conflict and chaos, whether external threat or inner turmoil. Psalm 84 is one that speaks especially of the peace that comes from 'dwelling' in the house, the 'dwelling-place', of God himself (vv. 1, 4, 10). With God as 'a sun and shield' (v. 11), this is a place of warmth and protection, a home that welcomes gentle, vulnerable creatures to its inner sanctuary (v. 3).

Psalm 27 also echoes the desire to 'dwell in the house of the Lord' as a place of safety and shelter (vv. 4–5), with room simply to sit and 'gaze' on his beauty. Similarly, in Psalm 91:1 we are promised that 'whoever dwells in the shelter of the Most High will rest in the shadow of the Almighty'. This rest, this peace, is not an absence of threat or conflict but a freedom from fear even when surrounded by danger, both day and night (vv. 5–7).

Before we run away with the idea, however, that the peace that comes from dwelling with or in God is a merely passive proposition—a snooze in the sun, or even a kind of hypnotic daze—we should note verses 5–6 of Psalm 84. The 'blessed' ones who dwell in God's house are also those 'whose hearts are set on pilgrimage'. They are on the move, allowing the peace of God to transform the bitter circumstances that they encounter (the Valley of Baka) into sources of refreshment.

In the teaching of Jesus, too, we find the same combination of rest and movement. He explained to his disciples how important it was to 'remain in me, as I remain in you' (John 15:4)—a mutual indwelling that provides the key to all fruitfulness and complete joy (v. 11). Yet he also spoke in terms of being 'yoked together' with him (Matthew 11:29–30) as co-workers. As someone who is overwhelmingly goal-focused, I find this a most helpful image. Yoked together with Jesus, we cannot charge ahead or lag behind; we are neither over-stressed nor lackadaisical. The arrangement works only if both partners are disciplined but at peace in each other's trusted company, walking at a steady pace. In this way, the goal of a well-ploughed field is achieved without panic or struggle.

3 Peace in practice

Philippians 4:1–9

In this short passage, Paul addresses several causes for a loss of peace of mind: quarrelling between colleagues; anxiety and negative thoughts; knowledge of what's right but a failure to act accordingly. We have no record of the specific disagreement between Euodia and Syntyche, but none of us will have any difficulty in listing a hundred and one types of conflict that it might have been, from our own experience of church, work and family life. Nor do we have any specific instructions from Paul as to how exactly the difficulty might be resolved—but perhaps his subsequent instructions (vv. 4–6) are of some help in the context of personal conflict as well as in the more general context that we might initially apply to them.

Suppose Euodia and Syntyche were asked to 'rejoice' together instead of complaining (v. 4)—to find something in their situation to laugh at or give thanks for. Suppose they were redirected into gentleness, where before they had shown only aggression or surliness towards one another. Suppose they were brought together to pray aloud about aspects of their joint labour that would usually keep them awake at night with anxiety. Might their disagreements then be on the way to resolution? Paul asks his 'true companion' (name unknown) to 'help' these women. Sometimes, an objective facilitator is needed to encourage and nurture warring parties (as well as anxious individuals) into a rejoicing, gentle, unworried attitude and mode of action. The 'peace of God, which transcends all understanding' (v. 7) might sound like a supernatural gift, but this passage suggests that it may be found by cultivating relatively simple, practical habits of thought.

The list of mentally uplifting qualities in verse 8 is worth studying in more detail. News headlines are not the place to start when looking for these attributes in everyday life. Scandal, misfortune and perceived dangers sell copy—but true, noble, right, pure, lovely, admirable, excellent and praiseworthy characteristics can all be identified in the people and events around us if we make a conscious decision to look out for them.

Finally, Paul urges his audience to 'put into practice' whatever they have learnt from him (v. 9). Our minds can become overloaded with information about the Christian life, from sermons or books or tapes. Peace often comes from doing just one thing instead of thinking about many.

4 Encounter on Mount Horeb

1 Kings 19:1–18

A threat to his life (v. 2) precipitates Elijah into a downward spiral of panic and despair, but this is only the climax to a violent and stressful series of events. His demonstration of God's dominance over the prophets of Baal has seen a full day of shouting and self-mutilation (18:28), animal and human slaughter (vv. 26, 40), the hard labour of building and digging (v. 32) and, lastly, a run of about 20 miles from Carmel to Jezreel (v. 46). No wonder he is exhausted enough simply to crumble at Jezebel's warning.

The rock-shattering wind, earthquake and fire that pass by Elijah on Mount Horeb could all be genuine expressions of God's presence and power (see Jeremiah 23:29; 30:23) but, on this occasion, the Lord chooses not to be 'in' these fierce elements. The preferred 'gentle whisper' (v. 12) is a difficult Hebrew phrase to translate. The King James version ('a still, small voice') is, perhaps, the best-known, but other renditions include 'a light murmuring sound' (NJB) and the paradoxical 'sound of sheer silence' (NRSV). Whichever comes closest to the original meaning, this barely audible representation of the true presence of the Lord finally brings Elijah the peace he has craved.

God's question is identical both before and after this experience (vv. 9, 13), as is Elijah's response. Objectively, nothing in the situation has changed, but, in Elijah's heart and mind, the complaints that had previously loomed so very large and real are now—perhaps even as he speaks (v. 14)—dwindling into mere shadows. At last, his mind is stilled, quiet enough to hear and obey a renewed commission: 'Go back the way you came…' (v. 15).

Theologian Maggi Dawn suggests that Elijah's victory on Mount Carmel was not the great triumph that it may have seemed, but was motivated by fear, insecurity and an exaggerated sense of isolation (*Beginnings and Endings*, BRF, 2007, pp. 55–57). Elijah, believing himself to be 'the only [prophet] left', leaps to defend God in a way that turns out to be unnecessary: there are, in fact, 7000 prophets of the Lord still active.

It is tempting, especially when we feel under siege, to be dragged into exhausting attempts to 'prove' the supremacy of our God. Even if our efforts seem successful, they can also be the precursor to collapse, if our perspective is not right. At these times, an encounter with the God who is 'not in' wind, earthquake and fire, but asks us to tune our ears in to a murmur, will restore peace of mind and bring a renewed sense of calling (vv. 15–16).

5 Futility and fruitfulness

Isaiah 55:8–11

Elijah won a 'victory' that did not bring him peace of mind; more often, our 'failures' have the same effect. Isaiah speaks here into a situation of futility, in which people are 'spending' and 'labouring' with no satisfaction (v. 2), and have closed their ears to God (v. 3).

There are times in our walk with God when we get locked in to circumstances that, despite our hard labour, grow more and more fruitless and confusing. It becomes impossible to discern God's guidance and we begin to panic. In our perplexity, we might cry with Job, 'If I go to the east... [or] the west, I do not find him. When he is at work in the north... [or] the south, I catch no glimpse of him' (23:8–9). If we are to regain peace of mind at those times when we have lost sight of God's purposes and are desperately looking to all four points of the compass without any sign of his presence, we need to stop, listen, and realise afresh that God's ways are far beyond our understanding (Isaiah 55:8–9: this, of course, is what Elijah also had to learn as the earthquake, wind and fire passed him by in 1 Kings 19:11–12).

It is perhaps puzzling that, after stressing the unfathomable distance between our ways and God's, Isaiah's prophecy should continue with an illustration that is so down to earth—that of plant growth (v. 10). Yet, even with our modern-day ability to manipulate so many factors, from soil fertility to the genetic structure of crops, the germination, growth and maturation of seeds depend heavily on the right weather conditions—something that is quite beyond our control and notoriously difficult to forecast.

We can understand the concept of seasonality in the cycle of planting and harvest: we sow and reap at the right times of year. God's purposes, Isaiah suggests, are also seasonal, though they may take longer to mature than we hope, and they may take a different form from what we expect.

Paul was aware, in the context of church growth, that 'I planted the seed, Apollos watered it, but God has been making it grow' (1 Corinthians 3:6; compare Jesus' kingdom parable in Mark 4:26–29). God, through Isaiah 55, encourages us to trust that the rain of his word 'will accomplish what I desire and achieve the purpose for which I sent it (v. 11). The result for us, then, is that we are 'led forth in peace'—into a time of refreshing new growth (vv. 12–13).

6 Call to action

1 Samuel 3

The previous five studies have explored various ways in which we can find peace of mind by realigning our thoughts. Today, however, we focus on the fact that we sometimes find our 'peace' challenged by God himself, in a call to action. It is often said that the Holy Spirit comforts the disturbed and disturbs the comfortable, so there may be a need for discernment to tell the difference between these two of his activities.

The young Samuel was comfortable enough, lying down to sleep in the sanctuary at Shiloh, but he was allowed no rest—literally—until he recognised and answered God's call. Next morning, Samuel was afraid to pass on the Lord's message to Eli but, again, found peace only when he had spoken out in obedience. When we are being called by God, peace does not always come easily, especially if we do not recognise his voice—or if we resist at first. Think of Jonah, fleeing in the opposite direction to Nineveh and bringing down a storm upon his head.

Are we like Samuel, trying to get some sleep when we are, in fact, being called repeatedly by God to serve him in some way? Is there a nagging urge to intercede for a person or situation, or a growing concern for mission in a challenging part of the country (or world)? Do we feel indignation rising inside us at the sight of a social injustice, with a conviction that something must be done? Maybe past hurts are refusing to stay buried, compelling us to seek healing and resolution.

Alternatively, we may identify more closely with Eli, who acted as mentor to the emerging prophet. Can we think of someone in our congregation or home group who is struggling to recognise and act upon a call from

God? We should note that Samuel 'did not yet know the Lord' (v. 7) but heard his voice, nonetheless. Perhaps we know someone who is not yet a believer but is being prompted to explore the claims of Christianity, and will find no peace until he or she does so. Is our role to encourage others to hear and respond?

God's call broke in on Samuel at a time when 'the word of the Lord was rare' (v. 1). Sometimes we can mistake the silence of God for peace, when it is only stagnation. Growth comes when we allow ourselves to be disturbed by his call.

Guidelines

'Seek peace and pursue it,' says 1 Peter 3:11 (quoting Psalm 34:14), and this is perhaps best done, in the first instance, through prayer. There may be one or more of this week's studies that have resonated especially with your own experience. If so, perhaps it would be helpful to spend some time simply 'dwelling' with God, confessing and receiving freedom from guilt and condemnation, or realigning your perspective with his on any number of different issues. Interpersonal conflicts, anxieties, negative thoughts, stress and confusion may all be brought to him in the search for 'the peace… which transcends all understanding'—and you may find that your understanding, as well as your peace, is deepened by his gentle whisper.

Next to prayer comes action. From the place of shelter and security with God, we work alongside him to answer his various calls to ministry. Is the gentle whisper sounding an insistent note in your ear, and, if so, how will you respond?

Holy Week to Easter:
'Love was his meaning'

Having made the journey through the weeks of Lent, that journey now intensifies as Jesus and his disciples have entered Jerusalem and we enter Holy Week. Depending upon the church we belong to, this can be a very busy week, with a number of services taking place each day, and unfolding each day something of the story that leads us to the cross.

During this first week, I hope to look at the stories of the passion from a prayerful and spiritual perspective, taking a quiet, reflective approach that may help to counter any sense of a busy rush from one service to another (not to mention preparations to celebrate the resurrection and Easter Day in church or with family). The second week will continue the story as we look at the transformation from grief and unbelief to joy and understanding, and the commissioning to discipleship.

The story of the passion and resurrection is familiar to us. When a story is so familiar, we can sometimes find ourselves missing the depth of meaning that lies within it, behind it and beyond it. It may simply touch only the surface of our being. Alternatively, because of personal circumstances and experiences, we may find ourselves entering into the passion narrative at a far greater depth than we expected to. We bring to it our own story. We journey into the darkness before we are lifted out into the light of a new beginning.

To bring our own story and experiences, present or from the past, can open up for us a pathway to a more profound experience of God with us, and into a more intimate relationship with the risen Christ. Through the weaving of our story into that of Jesus, it may reveal to us, as it was revealed to Julian of Norwich, the 13th-century anchoress and mystic, that 'Love was his meaning'.

As we look at the pain of betrayal and suffering, without love there is no meaning to all that took place, and only with love can there be any meaning to Good Friday. This is a love that becomes visible in the resurrection and through the stories of our lives and faith today.

All Bible quotations are taken from the New Revised Standard Version.

1 The preparation

Luke 22:7–15

We enter the story of the passion amid the noise of the crowds getting ready to celebrate the most important of Jewish festivals, the Passover. At the gathering at this festival, the story is retold of the liberation of their ancestors from the oppression of Pharaoh, the eventual coming home to the promised land, and all that they still wait for in faith.

The preparations for the Passover meal would have familiar to the disciples. After the overwhelming reception as they came into Jerusalem, they would no doubt be looking forward to the celebration, gathering together to eat the lamb, the bitter herbs and unleavened bread.

Unknown to the disciples, however, the story of this Passover would be transformed into a very different narrative, in which familiar events would take on a new depth of meaning as they were recounted from within the context of Jesus' own story—a story that would become theirs and ours. The annual repetition of the account of the exodus formed a part of their identity as Jews, and the sharing of the story would help to deepen its meaning within them and strengthen their faith.

How has sharing the story of your faith journey, and listening to the stories of others, helped to deepen its meaning for you?

How may you prepare yourself to hear the passion story with open and attentive ears, so that it may touch your life in new ways?

Peter and John are chosen by Jesus to go and prepare all that is needed for the celebration—a job usually left to the women or to slaves. This is not the only unusual aspect of the story, as soon they will find themselves challenged and confronted with the truth of the journey into Jerusalem, and will have to face up to their own inner weaknesses. Their story is about to take them in a very different direction from the one imagined when they first answered the call of Jesus to leave all behind and follow him.

The room has been found
and cushions are scattered around the table.

The lamb has been slaughtered and the table laid;
the wine is ready to be poured out, bread to be broken.
They await the arrival of the others. We wait…

2 The foot-washing

John 13:1–11

John's Gospel, full of contrasting imagery and symbolism, writes into the narrative here a dramatic change of tone. The story lifts off the page through the images it invokes as it describes this act of love, which was counter to Jewish culture: a teacher would not wash the feet of a student. Like the preparation for the meal, this very menial task would be left to the women or to a slave. Is this why the disciples reacted with such hesitancy and shock, or was it perhaps because of embarrassment at such intimate closeness with Jesus?

If foot-washing is a part of the liturgy of your Maundy Thursday, how comfortable or uncomfortable are you as feet are washed? How does it affect the way in which you relate to God?

Up to this point in the Gospel, Jesus has been the shepherd watching over the flock, teaching, nurturing, enabling and healing them. He drew to himself a rich and diverse group of people, offering them a new way of life, a new way of living out their own stories. He gave them the certainty and strength of his own story and being, which would help to hold them together in safety as they were encouraged to look deep within and see and believe in the transforming power of God. They were called to look upon this power of God, now made visible before them; but, as they did so, they discovered that it challenged all of their pre-imagined ideas about God. The God whom Jesus brought to them was very different.

Others heard, but only on the surface, and they left, not allowing his words to transform them or change their thoughts to grasp this new expression of God. Jesus' words hung in the air as he called them out from the darkness of unknowing and into the light of revelation. Even the disciples who were closest to Jesus struggled to understand fully the way of God as brought to them by Jesus, as we see in the reading. The God whom Jesus reveals is the God who intimately kneels, touches and washes feet.

Before the meal a bowl is brought, and filled with water.
Heads shake in shock, embarrassment,
as with intimate tenderness feet are lifted, washed, softly dried.
This is the touch of love. Feet are cleansed,
but does this cleansing love embrace the heart…?

3 The betrayal

Matthew 26:14–16, 20–25

A dark thread now weaves its way through this Holy Week narrative, a thread that touches the lives of more people than Judas Iscariot alone. The dark thread of betrayal is found in the story of some of the other disciples—in Peter's story as he denies knowing who Jesus is, in the scattering of other disciples in fear, and in their absence at the cross.

Betrayal may have reached out to touch your own life, making this reading difficult or painful. Has someone, or some group, betrayed you, let you down when you most needed their help or support, or spoken against you in some way? Is there someone you have betrayed? Within the context of the story of your life, what feelings arise when you read this passage?

Within the Gospels, and in relation to the action of Judas, some scholars argue that the word 'betray' has been mistranslated, and should instead be read as 'hand over'. The word 'betray' is a very powerful and emotive word to use, whereas 'hand over' has less initial impact: it sounds softer, less powerful, regardless of whether the outcome is the same. Do 'betrayed' and 'handed over' convey to you the same meaning, or different ones?

In the dialogue between Jesus and Judas, there is no sense that Jesus is judging Judas and what he is about to do. Rather, he allows Judas himself to make the final decision on how to act. Judas was responsible, as we are, for his own actions, and consequences that followed. In betraying or handing over Jesus, Judas may have acted out of impatience, wanting the kingdom of God to be brought in there and then; or his action may have stemmed from greed or from some other motive. The question to ponder over is how aware Judas was, at that moment, of the consequences of everything he was doing.

However we look at the complicated story of Judas, drawing into it

Peter's denial and the other disciples' desertion, there remains surrounding it the metanarrative of God's love.

Jesus looks at Judas, with eyes of love seeking to melt
the darkened heart, letting him go, wanting him back,
watching as the thread tightens its grip;
and so Judas leaves to earn his thirty pieces of silver.
The meal continues; do we stay…?

4 The meal

Mark 14:22–25

Mark briefly records the institution of the Lord's Supper, when Jesus takes the bread and wine of the Passover meal and gives them a new meaning.

A meal around a table is, or can be, an intimate time for the sharing of inner thoughts and the story of the day, a place to explore future hopes and dreams, a place to relax in companionable silence or with conversation and laughter. It is a time to be with family or friends. Think of a time when you have eaten a meal alone (which may be the case on most days) and of a time when you have shared a special meal with others. How did each experience feel, and how would you describe the difference between the two? If you could invite anyone to share a meal with you, who would they be?

The upper room is ready. The strangeness of having their feet washed by Jesus, and the questions raised about the possibility of betrayal, recede to the background of the disciples' thoughts as general conversation begins to take over—until the moment when Jesus speaks out. He lifts up the bread and gives thanks; then, breaking the bread, he passes it around the table. Pouring the wine, he does the same. As Jesus spoke, and the bread and wine were passed around, was there a change in the the mood at the table? Did the disciples feel within themselves the importance of that moment, of all that Jesus was saying and doing?

On this night, we gather to celebrate the Passover meal, now transformed into the Lord's Supper. We come to eat the bread and drink the wine before the vigil of watching and waiting begins. After hearing the story, how does it feel to receive the love and grace of God, given to us in bread and wine, on this particular night? As the story takes us from the meal to the garden of Gethsemane, what have been the watching and waiting times in your journey of faith and in your day-to-day life?

Reclining around the table, the food
is taken, blessed and shared, passed from one to another.
Words are spoken in remembrance of the past, words transformed
to tell a new story for the future, words embracing now the light and
the shadows of the room. Outside, a garden waits…

5 The cross

Matthew 27:32–44

The arrest of Jesus, Peter's denial of him, and the meeting and trial before Herod and Pilate have taken place, and we join the story as we walk with Jesus to the place of pain and suffering. It is a place that is difficult to approach, to contemplate the violence that one human being can afflict upon another. The agony of the crucifixion can be felt as we read, or hear read, this part of the passion narrative. We may close our eyes to the scene, when portrayed on TV or in a film. We may shy away from it, and yet, on this day, it is where we are called to be—at the foot of the cross.

Matthew is very matter-of-fact in the way he records the events, keeping to the details without giving any space to linger upon the emotional and spiritual torment taking place. Yet, in recording the actions of the soldiers and the mocking of the bandits, he draws them unwittingly in as witnesses to the story, purpose and plan of God. He lifts their words and actions out of the darkness of disbelief and unknowing, into the light of truth. The truth is before them, though they cannot see it, that the one they deride is the Son of God, the Messiah.

Julian of Norwich sought to feel in her own body something of Christ's passion, and was granted the experience. She writes in her *Revelations of Divine Love*, 'And at once I saw the red blood trickling down from under the garland, hot, fresh, and plentiful, just as it did at the time of his blessed passion when the crown of thorns was pressed on the blessed head of God-and-Man, who suffered for me' (Penguin Classics, 1966, p. 211).

This may not be the experience we seek, but how do we pray on this day? What is your prayer as you kneel before, or look upon, the cross?

Is it a place where the burdens you carry can be laid down, where you can seek forgiveness and feel God's love? Is it a place to seek a deeper understanding and awareness of all that Christ suffered? Is it a place of self-offering into God's service?

Lifted high, and battered by nails and mocking voices,
the smell of sweat, blood and sour wine pervades,
and the desolating forsakenness begins to darken the sky
as active Love slows into passivity with each
struggling, dying, breath…

6 The silence

Luke 23:50–56

Into the silence following the death that shook the earth and tore the veil in the temple, Luke brings Joseph of Arimathea. Joseph, a member of the Sanhedrin, is assumed not to have been present when the others consented to the crucifixion of Jesus. Luke describes him as one 'waiting expectantly for the kingdom of God' (v. 51), and again it can be assumed that he had heard Jesus speak and, in his own way, was a follower. It must have taken personal conviction and courage for Joseph to go to Pilate and ask permission to take the body of Jesus from the cross.

With care, Joseph takes the body of Jesus, wraps it in the cloths he has brought and lays it in an empty tomb. The women have gathered and prepared the spices and ointments in readiness to complete his body for burial; now they wait, for 'on the sabbath they rested according to the commandment' (v. 56b).

Everything stops. Creation holds its breath as the activity of love, present even in the passivity of this waiting silence, becomes still, unseen. Waiting is never easy, regardless of what we are waiting for. Yet, as W.H. Vanstone wrote in *The Stature of Waiting*, 'The experience of waiting is the experience of the world as in some sense *mattering*, as being of some kind of importance' (p. 103, italics in original).

We wait as Joseph, the women and the male disciples did, because it matters to us, is important to us, not to forget this Holy Saturday, as can easily happen. Today we are called, too, to embrace the silence.

As the day progresses, the silence will slowly recede as our churches prepare for the day of resurrection. The transformation begins to take place, with flowers, an Easter garden, the lighting of the Paschal candle, and the sound of music at the Easter Vigil, welcoming in this new day as the next part of the story waits to be told.

Enclosed, hidden from sight, lies the body, lifeless, wrapped with care,
and the world rests in a tense uneasy silence.
Waiting silently, the anointing spices and ointments prepared,
Love is quiet, still, until a faint glow of light is seen in the east,
as the sun slowly begins to rise...

Guidelines

Julian of Norwich wrote that 'Love was his meaning', and on this day we can perhaps now see this meaning more clearly as we gather to celebrate and rejoice in the resurrection. Without love there can be no meaning to anything. On this day of new beginnings and the realisation of forgiveness and salvation, we can also hear the words, again from Julian of Norwich, that now 'all shall be well'.

From the pain and darkness of Holy Week, we move into the light of life itself. Next week we see how the resurrection touched the lives of those who knew Jesus, and we reflect on how knowing Jesus touches the story of who we are.

The Light of dawn slowly transforms the new day,
as Love bursts through the tomb of darkness and death,
and Light fills the land.
The silent desolation is shattered,
and the music of life itself rises in a crescendo,
for the Son is risen.
Alleluia!

1 Joy

John 20:11–18

The resurrection account in John's Gospel is a story told in connecting parts. First there is the discovery of the empty tomb and the race between Peter and the beloved disciple (20:1–10). Next comes the passage we look at today, which is followed by the appearance of Jesus in the upper room that same evening (vv. 19–23).

There is a movement in each part, and overall, from grief and unbelief, or disbelief, towards a growing sense of joy as the truth of the resurrection is finally seen and believed. There is movement in the garden as Mary turns, and turns again in response to the man she cannot yet see as the risen Jesus. With each turn, the conversation deepens, yet in her grief the truth remains hidden. She stays, though, still seeking, wanting to know where the body is. We can assume that Mary is alone in the garden with no witnesses to her meeting with Jesus, whom she sees as a gardener. Later, she will go, having been sent to the disciples to share with them, witness to them, the news that Christ is risen.

In Jewish culture at that time, women could not give testimony or be witnesses. To be valid, any witness or testimony had to come from two men. Yet it is Mary, not Peter or the other disciple, who is sent by Jesus to witness to the resurrection. As we read in Mark 16:11 and Luke 24:11, the disciples didn't believe her when she told them the good news. They believed and rejoiced only after they had witnessed with their own eyes. Joy could be felt only after they had made the journey through grief and finally realised the truth.

Joy comes to Mary when Jesus calls her by her name, and only then does she recognise who is standing before her. In naming her, Jesus establishes a new relationship with her, as he does with us, knowing and calling us by our own name; as we read in Isaiah 43:1, 'I have called you by name'. Called by name into this new relationship, Mary is then sent to witness, as today we too are sent out to witness through our own lives.

Where and how is the joy felt, known and expressed in and through your relationship with God?

2 Understanding

Luke 24:13–35

On the road to Emmaus, we encounter the confusion of grief mixed with the possibility of hope. The disciples walk despondently, not knowing what to make of all that has taken place that day. Is Jesus alive? Is it true, or is it simply a story? As they walk and talk in the darkening evening, Jesus comes alongside them. As Mary had not recognised Jesus the same morning, the two disciples also fail to recognise him. He joins them and enters into their story, meeting them where they are at that precise moment, and, opening up the scriptures, he begins to reveal who he is.

Reflecting afterwards, they come to understand the meaning of the warmth they felt within as the stranger, Jesus, spoke to them. At the time, the truth was hidden from their inner and outer sight. The truth comes to them with a gesture, a gesture that must have been familiar to them. They sit together to share a meal, when the stranger takes, blesses, breaks and gives to them the bread that is on the table. At that moment, they see and know and understand. At that moment of realisation and understanding, Jesus disappears!

Augustine, in his early fifth-century work *The Trinity*, used the phrase 'faith seeks, understanding finds'. In the eleventh century, the medieval theologian Anselm shortened this to 'faith seeking understanding', to refer to the search for understanding in faith by the use of reason.

In our Christian journey, as we grow in faith, we seek to deepen our understanding. We enter into a spiral effect: as our understanding grows, so does our faith, and we therefore need to seek more understanding to help us develop and continue to grow in faith. We see this in the two disciples on the road to Emmaus; can you see it in yourself?

How do you recognise the presence of God with you, day by day, and in the special moments of your life? The two disciples came to understand, and so believe, the news of the resurrection through the familiar action of the breaking of the bread. How does the receiving of the bread of Communion help you to understand something more of the Christian faith?

3 Peace

'Peace be with you.' Before those words are spoken by Jesus, there seems to be little peace in the room where the disciples are gathered. The disciples are fearful, and the doors are locked and bolted. Is this fear a reaction to the arrest and crucifixion of Jesus, or to the news that Mary Magdalene brought to them about the resurrection?

Into the fear held within the room, Jesus comes, without knocking at the door or waiting to be let in. The well-known painting *The Light of the World*, by Holman Hunt (1827–1910), evocatively portrays Jesus standing and waiting to be allowed entry. The door is closed as he knocks, a door that can only be opened from the inside, by ourselves. The outside of the door is overgrown by plants and weeds. With light in hand, Jesus waits.

In their fear, the disciples would have been unlikely to open the door, had he knocked, so Jesus comes and stands in the middle of them, startling them as he makes his presence known, speaking and offering them his peace. He gives his peace to them without questioning their actions over the previous few days, without judging their unbelief. He simply lets them see the physical wounds in his hands and side. As they look, they see and know and believe. As they then rejoice, Jesus offers his peace into their rejoicing.

There is a deeper message within these words of peace. Firstly, to know the peace of God leads to a sending out in faith, to share that peace with others. Secondly, out of this peace comes an awareness of forgiveness—both of being forgiven and of the need to forgive others. Thirdly, in the giving of his peace, Jesus draws this group of frightened disciples together and, transforming them with his unconditional love and peace, he prepares them for the ministry that each one will discover as their calling.

In your own story, how have you known, or been made aware of, these three elements of God at work in the journey of life and faith? How may you share something of the peace of God with others today? How do you know and feel God's peace within you?

134   25 April–1 May

4 Belief

There was one person missing from our reading and reflection yesterday. Where was Thomas? If the disciples were locked inside the room out of fear, what was so important that Thomas had left them, and the safety of that room, to venture outside? Had he perhaps needed to be alone in his grief? These are questions to ponder and speculate over.

When Thomas returns, he doesn't believe what the others tell him. He can't 'see' the truth in their words. As they had wanted, so he too wants actual and visual proof—to see Jesus with his own eyes and touch him with his own hands. Thomas has to wait a whole week before he is granted his desire.

Again, Jesus appears in their midst and offers his words of peace to everyone. He then invites Thomas to touch the wounds in his hands and side, and to feel the life that is in him. How long did they stand looking at each other before Thomas spoke? How quiet and still were the other disciples at that moment, waiting and watching?

Thomas, very simply but also very profoundly, speaks straight from his heart: 'My Lord and my God!' (v. 28). There is no need to touch. Out of his doubt comes an unwavering confession of belief.

Only Thomas is traditionally described as 'doubting', and yet the other disciples gathered in that room had also doubted before seeing Jesus for themselves. The Victorians used the phrase 'honest doubt', meaning to be honest about things that we struggle to understand, those aspects of our faith that we find difficult to relate to within the contradictions of society and the aggression of the world. Some may say that to doubt shows a lack of faith. We often find, though, that our times of doubt, the questioning of our faith, can open the way to discerning a deeper truth of God in the story of our lives, through which we then grow in faith.

When you look back on the story of your faith journey, have there been times of doubt? How have you grown in faith and belief through that experience?

5 Renewal

John 21:15–19

The disciples are together again with Jesus, sharing a meal—and a very different meal from the one they shared at the last supper. This time it is a relaxed picnic breakfast on the beach with bread and fish cooked over a fire. It is a meal that Jesus prepares for the disciples after the busyness of their work. The story after the meal is also very different: there is no garden of Gethsemane, but a one-to-one conversation between Jesus and Peter.

Peter was known for being impetuous—jumping in with both feet, often speaking without thinking too much about the consequences of what he said—but also for being a man of faith. Yet, at the time of the passion, he revealed his inner fears and weaknesses, which made him vulnerable despite all of his outer show of strength and confidence. Having denied Jesus three times, Peter is now asked by Jesus if he loves him, not once but three times. It is a very different Peter who answers. Aware of all that he has said and hasn't said, he answers simply, perhaps even hesitantly, but with honesty and truthfulness. Pleading to be believed, Peter declares his love.

In his declaration there is forgiveness—albeit not mentioned as such—and renewal, as Jesus commissions Peter to the ministry that is now his, a calling to live and die as Jesus did. The renewal of Peter is established further as Jesus says to him, 'Follow me'.

In following, Peter becomes, out of and in spite of his weaknesses, the rock upon which the Church will be built. The same Church continues to be built as Jesus renews his call today, to us, to 'follow me'. Peter is called by Jesus to be a shepherd for the flock, to care for them, nurture them in the faith and feed their spiritual hunger. This is something that he can do only through the strength and empowerment that come from his love of Jesus. Out of all of our weaknesses and limitations, we too are called to follow, which sets us free from seeking an unattainable perfection and releases us to be true to our own selves.

In the story of your life, when and how have you heard the call of Jesus to follow him, and how did you answer? Where and how have you felt a sense of renewal in your relationship with God?

6 Calling

Matthew 28:16–20

Julian of Norwich sought to understand the meaning that lay within the visions granted to her by God. She had felt the suffering of the crucified Christ, acknowledged the sinfulness of humanity, and recognised through faith that beyond it all, sustaining her and all creation, was love, for 'Love was his meaning'. She knew, too, that it was because of God's love for her that this understanding was revealed to her through the visions.

Love has been the foundation of the story we have entered into over these past two weeks. The love of God is seen weaving its way through the accounts of betrayal and denial, through the grief, fear and unbelief, and into rejoicing and the renewal of belief. This is a love that now calls and commissions the disciples into their future discipleship, and it is a love that calls out to us today.

We began Holy Week with Jesus sending the disciples out to prepare the room for the Passover meal. Jesus now prepares to send the disciples out into the world, preparing them for his departure, too. As they gather on the mountain, they worship, and yet for some the seeds of doubt remain (v. 17). Regardless of their doubt, Jesus commissions them, knowing that they can and will fulfil their calling to go out and baptise, teach and make disciples.

Answering the call to follow draws us all into the life of Jesus, and enables us to make Jesus present within the world, in and through the context and place where we live and work, in and through the context and place of our calling. Our calling needs to be discerned, to be called out from the story of our life, our faith and our giftedness. That calling may or may not be to a specific ministry or area of service within the church or community. Always, though, it is to be a person who shares and makes visible the love of God.

How have you heard the call of Jesus? Do you feel that you are being called to something new? As Jesus reassured the disciples, so we too have the same reassurance for our own calling: 'I am with you always, to the end of the age' (v. 20).

Guidelines

Over the past two weeks, we have turned the pages of the story of faith from the passion to the resurrection, from darkness to light. In the resurrection and the slowly dawning belief of the disciples, we see not only the love of God and the meaning which is Love, but also Julian of Norwich's well-known assurance that 'all shall be well'.

All shall be well because of God's love for us, no matter how difficult life may become at times, or however much we may doubt or fear. God's love enters into our own personal story and calls us to follow new and different storylines for the chapters yet to be written. Maybe that is something that is already being revealed to you.

FURTHER READING

Julian of Norwich, *Revelations of Divine Love*, Penguin Classics, 1966.

Jean Vanier, *Drawn into the Mystery of Jesus through the Gospel of John*, DLT, 2004.

W.H. Vanstone, *Fare Well in Christ*, DLT, 1997.

W.H. Vanstone, *The Stature of Waiting*, DLT, 1994.

The BRF

Magazine

Richard Fisher writes...

By the time you read this, I hope you'll already be aware that 2011 marks the 400th anniversary of the publication of the King James Version (KJV) of the Bible. It promises to be a very significant year for BRF and, indeed, everyone involved in Bible ministry of all kinds, with the anniversary prompting a year-long celebration of the Bible in English.

While we're involved in general terms with the initiatives being championed by both The 2011 Trust (www.2011trust.org.uk) and BibleFresh (www.biblefresh.com), BRF is making a key contribution through our Barnabas in Schools team. We believe 2011 provides a unique opportunity for teachers and children in primary schools to revisit the widespread impact of the Bible on life in the UK. The Bible's significant contribution in the fields of literature, art, music, politics, education, morals and the laws of our land can't be overestimated. This amounts to a compelling educational reason for exploring and celebrating its importance during this anniversary year.

Under the title 'What's so special about the Bible?' we're offering a new resource to schools. This includes a new INSET session for teachers, looking at what sort of book the Bible is and ways to use the Bible creatively in the classroom; a new, interactive Barnabas RE Day for children, using a range of creative arts that explore the Christian's special book; and publication of a set of free resources (including a handbook entitled *The People's Bible* and a DVD) that provide lesson outlines, ideas for collective worship and project material.

The INSET session has been available since September 2010, when the new academic year began, and the RE Day is available to schools throughout 2011. Our hope is to enable even more teachers and primary school children than ever to explore what's so special about the Bible during the year ahead.

Please pray especially for the Barnabas in Schools team during 2011. Take a look at the 2011 Trust and BibleFresh websites, where you will find the latest news about all that's going on, and do encourage your own church to get involved. It's going to be an exciting year!

Richard Fisher, Chief Executive

Messy Church migrates

Lucy Moore

The freezing weather in the UK at the beginning of 2010 made me realise why swallows whizz off to the south, and why so many Brits buy homes in a climate that doesn't require the wearing of vests. Of course, one issue for ex-pats and swallows alike is the thorny one of settling into the new place and making it home—how closely to stick with your own habits and how much to change to fit the surrounding culture. It's interesting to think of Messy Church in this context, too. How much should it try to stay the same wherever it goes and how much should it adapt to local situations?

In February 2010, I joined the Archdeaconry of Gibraltar at their Synod in the Algarve. I have to confess to knowing very little about the Diocese of Europe apart from exotic adverts in the *Church Times* asking for vicars in places like Tenerife or Casablanca—which would be thrust under my husband Paul's nose with pleas that he might be called to somewhere similarly sunny next time we move. It hasn't happened yet. But at the Synod, there were people with name badges that together would have formed the best part of a Thompson's holiday brochure: Gibraltar, Canaries, Malaga, Barcelona... It was very hard not to squeal excitedly at everyone and tell them how lucky they are.

However, it's not always easy to be a vicar of these highly individual congregations. Congregation members of a chaplaincy are often quite elderly, may be away in other parts of the world for long periods, and can be widely scattered, having to travel miles to their nearest Anglican church. A minister might manage only one visit to a parishioner in an afternoon, as distances are so huge. Certainly communications and face-to-face meetings across an area that stretches from northern Spain to northern Africa (and that's just one archdeaconry) are a challenge.

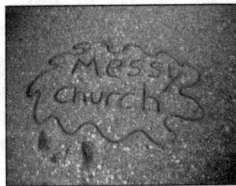

I had the enormous privilege of presenting Messy Church to the Synod. As I'd been up since 2 a.m. to catch a plane, I don't know that I was at my peak, but everyone was very interested and responsive. I doubt that pipe cleaners have often been seen at Synod meetings in the past, and in an hour we covered a lot of ground, inviting discussion about the whole Fresh Expressions movement and the principles and practice of Messy Church itself. I got the impression that, even though the idea of Messy Church appealed to many people who have a great heart for families of ex-pats, it would need considerable rethinking to work in this different context. It will be interesting to see if there are any developments once Synod members have had time to report back to their respective churches. If nothing else, I was able to assure them of our prayers for them and ask them for their prayers for Messy Churches and for BRF.

After the Synod, I enjoyed a weekend with a BRF supporter on the Costa del Sol in Spain, leading a Messy Fiesta in her chaplaincy and preaching in church. It made me feel very close to our BRF network of readers spread out across the world, and very appreciative of belonging to this wonderful worldwide family of Christ. It also reinforced for me how much we need to pray for each other as we all struggle with different pressures and relish different joys.

Could Messy Church be seen as an ex-pat of the sort (and I don't think I met any in Portugal or Spain, so perhaps they're a myth) who clings to The One Great British Way of Doing Things and refuses to have anything to do with Local Culture? I don't think it can be. One thing we've seen over and over again with the different Messy Churches popping up is the way it can be contextualised to work best in the place where it is being developed. While I would say that there are certain givens if an expression of church is going to be called Messy Church—that it's all-age, that it's for people who don't belong to another form of church, and that it's based on hospitality, creativity and celebration—it does seem to be infinitely adaptable. Revd George Lings of the Sheffield Centre wrote:

Messy Church is important within the current re-imagination of what it is to be Church. Don't dumb it down to kids, crafts and church-lite. It fosters inherent participation by contrast to congregational passivity. It connects across the generations instead of 'sending the children out'.

It offers a holistic vision of church by weaving together community and creativity, out of which comes appropriate liturgy. This is positively different from laying on worship into which the attenders are assimilated. Moreover, its spread shows it is accessible and transferable to many contexts. It has much to teach us all. (My emphasis)

It's most exciting where imaginative and sensitive changes have been made to work in a specific setting: out in the marketplace in Liverpool, on the beach in Cornwall, or in a school in Bristol. As Messy Church appears in different countries, it is fascinating to see how it meets the needs of families across the globe, and to ponder how we can learn from our brothers and sisters overseas.

The changes in technology mean that the far-flung limbs of the body of Christ can be linked not just through prayer but through the lifeblood of communication, too. As I'm writing this, I've stopped for 25 minutes to have a Skype call with Debbie Smith in New Zealand. It's 9.30 a.m. here and 10.30 p.m. there—all very surreal, and yet her voice speaking right into my study makes their joys and problems very real. Debbie is coordinating Messy Church for us in New Zealand and is keeping us in touch with the various Messy initiatives that are growing out there. She meets regularly with Jo Latham from Christchurch, who has probably been running her Families @ 4 Messy Church longer than anyone on that side of the world. Jo Skyped recently, too, about the developments they've been making with regard to discipleship:

We struggle with it too. One thing that developed last year was a small coffee morning for four of the mums with their kids who are really getting to know each other and talk together about life issues. Our hope is to gently introduce a low-key study with a grandma who is going to share her story with them first. Another little development that has grown out of the desire to build community among the parents is a home group on a Sunday lunchtime once a month for the whole family, where the kids will be occupied while the parents have a study-cum-discussion, and then on another evening a study for those who are further on the journey. And there's a blokes' event that has helped them get to know each other. All small, with lots of time and energy to grow.

In Canada, our dear Regional Coordinators, Thomas Brauer and Andy and Sue Kalbfleisch, have been enthusiastically sharing the ideas with churches there and working with Fresh Expressions to build up the Messy Churches. Sue reckons there are at least eight in Eastern Canada already, and we know of others right over to the Diocese of Westminster in the west. They grow in a haphazard way, as and when people hear about them, mostly through word of mouth, much as has been happening in the UK.

In Denmark, however, the Lutheran Church read about Messy Church in the book, then got excited enough to have the book translated and to get a website designed and in place before a single Danish Messy Church existed. Bjarne Gertz Olsen was delighted to tell us of three that have started up in the four months since the launch of the book, all encouraged by the Church from the centre.

In South Africa, one lone Messy Church operates, the organiser having heard of it through her contacts in England. Jean Pienaar wrote:

Our Messy Christmas went off remarkably well in December, and all the people (young and old) enjoyed themselves more than they thought they would! It was intentional to keep it small, especially as a 'trial run', and we had about 25 folk enjoy the afternoon. Our schools broke up for their summer holiday at the beginning of December, and traditionally Johannesburg is extremely quiet at that time of the year, as everyone flocks to the coast, or home. Most who attended were directly linked to the parish, but we felt that we also needed to let our own parishioners 'taste' the experience so that they can invite friends next time.

In the States, a Messy Church happens occasionally (and hugely) near Boston, where their Christmas service involved packing 187 gift bags to take round to the city's homeless people.

God's love is the same yesterday, today and for ever; the ways we express his love can change from generation to generation, Messy Church being one of the most recent expressions. The ways we support each other, from Newfoundland to Newquay, are both ancient and modern: through Skype and emails, but also through the tried-and-tested faithful prayer of God's people, one for another. So, once again, thank you for your prayers for BRF as we continually seek God's will and wisdom in reaching out through Messy Church and all the other wonderful ways God has given us to draw people of all ages closer to him.

Lucy Moore heads up BRF's Messy Church ministry. For more information, visit www.messychurch.org.uk.

Working for the Barnabas children's ministry team

Jane Butcher

'A week in the life of Barnabas' is a difficult thing to explain. There really aren't any two weeks that are the same—and that, for me, is part of the enjoyment of the role. A week's work can vary from being in school, leading creative RE days with primary school children, to being invited to the launch of the BRF/ Jerusalem Trust Paperless Christmas at Lambeth Palace.

It's hard to say which is the most enjoyable aspect of the work. The choices are many and varied—schools work with children, INSET training with teachers, church-based and Messy Church training, being involved with seminars at conferences, networking with other organisations, writing articles and books... and so the list could continue. Every aspect is rewarding in its own way. It is a privilege to hear a child sharing something from his or her faith journey, and equally rewarding to see teachers feeling renewed and enthused after a training day. Likewise, it's encouraging to see church-based leaders feeling equipped for their (often voluntary) role and parents being assured that others are facing the same situations as they do.

Are there challenges? As in so many roles, the answer is 'Yes'. At a practical level, there might be an early morning motorway journey to a fairly distant of the country to reach a school by 8.15am, with the journey home after a long, intensive day of being on your feet. However, one thing can always be guaranteed, and that is the support and encouragement of our fellow team members. We may often be working at opposite ends of the country but the prayer and practical support we receive from one another, and from our many supporters, make a big difference.

We are also aware of the need to keep in touch with what is happening in schools and churches, so that we can tailor our resources to fulfil national requirements, while offering enough flexibility to meet needs that may be specific to a particular church or school setting. Recently, we have seen a rise in the number of requests from churches for longer-term 'consultancy' support, which we have begun to provide.

There are most definitely some exciting things happening. Children's ministry never remains static, and we are grateful for that. We ourselves are developing new packages for our RE days and offering new training sessions for teachers, including Quiet Days, which provide the chance to reflect, both professionally and personally. Messy Church continues to grow in new and exciting ways, having now reached as far afield as Canada, Denmark and South Africa.

Another area of work that has been emerging for us recently is 'faith in the home'. There is a growing awareness among many Christian organisations committed to working with children and families that the development of faith in the home does not always receive the attention it deserves. Maybe this is because the church's programmes are focused on other areas, or because faith development is assumed to be the role of the church and children's Sunday groups. But faith grows over time through the whole of life's experience, with all the joys and challenges we encounter along the way.

The Barnabas children's ministry team recognises the need to develop ways of supporting parents, carers and children in their own homes. We seek to offer practical ways to encourage, empower and equip them to work out what it means to be a Christian family in the everyday routines of life. We are committed to researching this area, developing appropriate resources and providing ongoing support for parents' and children's spiritual journey beyond Sunday.

However, we are also increasingly aware of the time pressures that families face, juggling work, school and after-school activities. We know that people are hesitant to embark on programmes that will only add more hours of commitment to an already overstretched family life. For that reason, we want to encourage families to experience 'God in the everyday'. We are seeking to do this with those who have an established Christian faith and want to nurture it at home, as well as the increasing number of people who have not grown up with any experience of the Christian faith and those who just beginning to encounter faith through fresh expressions of church such as Messy Church.

If you are interested in this area of our work, do take the opportunity to look at the Barnabas in Churches website, www.barnabasinchurches. org.uk, and select the Faith at Home tab.

Jane Butcher is a member of the Barnabas children's ministry team, and is based in the Midlands.

Recommended reading

Naomi Starkey

A momentous anniversary falls in 2011: the 400th anniversary of the King James Version (also known as the Authorised Version) of the Bible. It is four centuries since this translation was first published, with the intention of providing a dignified and authoritative English Bible suitable for both public worship and private prayer.

While a great many English translations have appeared since 1611, the King James Version (KJV) remained for generations the most important Protestant version of the Bible and has also profoundly shaped both English language and literature. It is only fitting, therefore, that BRF should mark this anniversary—not least because the KJV is still widely used and loved around the world today. Published in conjunction with the 2011 Trust (established to celebrate the legacy of the KJV), *Celebrating the King James Version* offers short devotional readings by *New Daylight* contributor Rachel Boulding. Drawing from both Old and New Testaments, she writes to help the reader reflect on the richness and resonance of the language.

Rachel also demonstrates that, far from being a 'cultural artefact' or museum piece, this unique and beautiful translation of the Bible continues to speak to us today as we seek to follow God. *Celebrating the King James Version* is primarily designed to be used for daily reflection, but also includes an afterword by Professor Alison Shell of Durham University on the cultural and historical significance of the translation.

Learning to appreciate how the original writers of scripture shaped their text to convey its message, as well as absorbing the message itself, is a significant factor in deepening understanding of how the Bible 'works'. *Meditating with Scripture: John's Gospel* by Elena Bosetti, the first BRF book focused on the ancient tradition of *lectio divina* ('sacred reading'), enhances our appreciation of what many would consider to be the most carefully structured and lyrically written of all the Gospel accounts.

The *lectio divina* way of reading scripture is rooted in an approach that does not separate reason from faith or the intellect from the heart. While understanding the original context is important, fundamental to *lectio divina* is a prayerful listening, under the guiding presence of the Holy Spirit, to what the text is saying to us here and now. *Meditating with Scripture* makes this 'dialogue with the word' accessible to readers, combining exposition of the Gospel text with helpful exercises at the end of each chapter, together with concluding meditations to help shape a personal response. The book has been warmly endorsed by Canon David Winter, who writes, 'This is as persuasive an introduction as one could get to… a way of reading the Bible that lets the sacred text speak directly to heart and mind.'

A meditative reading of scripture is also a feature of another BRF book, *The Promise of Easter* by Fleur Dorrell. This is a companion volume to Fleur's very popular *The Promise of Christmas: Reflections for the Advent Season*, which BRF published in 2007. Like her earlier book, *The Promise of Easter* is published in conjunction with the Mothers' Union, where Fleur works as Head of Faith & Policy. Her role involves enriching MU members in their faith and spirituality and campaigning on social justice and faith issues affecting women and families worldwide.

The Promise of Easter offers non-dated Bible readings and reflections following the themes of holiness, relationship, forgiveness, sacrifice, hope and love, designed to be read primarily during the weeks of Lent. Fleur shows that although such themes are relevant at any time of year, they gain a particular resonance in the Lenten season when we have a particular call to engage with the mysteries of Christ's suffering. Such engagement will bring us closer to our Lord and Saviour, transforming us so that we too may find ourselves willing to offer ourselves in self-sacrificial love to the world. In so doing, we pray that the world in turn will glimpse a little of the true significance of the events of Easter.

Finally, it is exciting to be able to report a further development for a central component of BRF's publishing programme. *The People's Bible Commentary* series was completed in 2006 with Loveday Alexander's volume on the book of Acts, and the series is now established as an important resource for those involved in preaching and teaching the Bible, for first-time students of the Bible, and for those who want to venture into more in-depth study of a passage than is possible with daily Bible reading notes. A number of the New Testament volumes— the four Gospels, plus Acts and 1 and 2 Corinthians—have now been republished as new editions, complete with attractively redesigned covers, to help commend the books to an even wider audience than before.

Naomi Starkey is Editor of New Daylight *and Commissioning Editor for BRF's range of adult books. To order copies of her recommended books, please turn to the order form on page 159.*

An extract from
Jesus Christ—the Alpha & the Omega

As we pass through the weeks of Lent, the crucified Christ increasingly fills our gaze. However, in order to grasp more fully the scope and significance of his supreme sacrifice, we need to embrace and believe in the whole Christ, Alpha to Omega. In this, the BRF Lent book for 2011, author Dr Nigel G. Wright takes us on two journeys: an extended exploration of the person and work of Jesus Christ, and a journey of devotion and discipleship through the events of Holy Week. The first two readings in the book (both based on John 1:1–18) are extracted below.

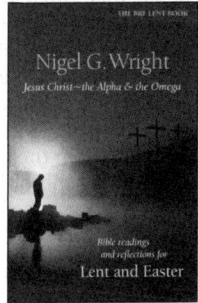

Christ the key to all things

And the Word became flesh and lived among us, and we have seen his glory, the glory as of a father's only son, full of grace and truth (v. 14).

A few years ago, I was a speaker at Easter People, the Bible Week initiated by the late Rob Frost. They organisers decided to put me in the alternative venue, where the idea was to do things differently, with more of a performing arts emphasis. The brains behind this venue came up with a new idea. On stage they erected a Christmas tree made of coat hangers. Every speaker was supposed to suspend something from the tree and then talk about it for a full minute without hesitation, deviation or repetition. This was fine, except that they forgot to tell the speakers that this was going to happen. So there we were, scrabbling around in our baggage for something to hang from the tree.

The speaker before me was Adrian Plass, who hung up his toothbrush. I have forgotten now what exactly he said about it but I do remember the toothbrush. Then it was my turn. All I had with me was a bunch of car keys. Inspiration struck: Jesus Christ is the key that unlocks the mysteries of the universe. That, it seems to me, is the great theme that runs through these magnificent first 18 verses of John's Gospel, which are sometimes called the 'Prologue' to John's Gospel. That astonishing belief in Jesus, it equally seems to me, is what lies at the very heart of the Christian faith.

Today we begin a journey together. We do so on [Ash Wednesday], a day that marks the beginning of a pilgrimage Christians take every year, at least in their minds—a journey to Jerusalem, to the cross and to the empty tomb of Jesus. The purpose of our journey is to understand how Christ can be the key to the mysteries of the universe. We shall do this by recalling who Christ is and the journey that he has first made towards us, which precedes any journey that we can make towards him. It is a journey from eternity into time and then from time into eternity. In the church's language, we sometimes speak of God's 'prevenient grace'. By this we mean that Christianity is not, first and foremost, a religion that tells of how we can reach up to God but one that speaks of how God has reached down to us. God has gone before us, coming to us in love and grace in order that we might find him as he draws near. If we ever reach out to God and seek him, it is because his love first prompts us and enables us to do so. Salvation is of the Lord. It comes as a gracious gift from God, as does everything that is good, true and beautiful.

> *The greatest mystery is the mystery of God himself*

What does it mean for Christ to unlock the mysteries of the universe? The greatest mystery is the mystery of God himself. How can finite and sinful human beings speak of God? God is infinitely great, greater than the universe itself, in which there are said to be ten billion galaxies, each containing ten billion stars. By comparison with them, we are so small and insignificant. Our minds and imaginations are all the more puny by contrast with the God who exceeds them all. We might as well seek to contain the oceans in a bucket. We cannot speak of God because, on our own, we have no way of knowing God, no way of unlocking the mystery of God's own being. But there is a key to that mystery and it is Jesus Christ, the one who appears in John's Gospel as 'the Word of God'. 'In the beginning was the Word, and the Word was with God, and the Word was God' (1:1). 'The Word became flesh and lived among us, and we have seen his glory' (v. 14). This is how the Christian can begin to speak of God, because God has first of all spoken to us in a Son who has come to us, clothed in our flesh and living our life.

Jesus is the Word of God. What do we use words for? One way we use them is to express ourselves. Every speaker—perhaps every singer, too—knows that there is something very satisfying about expressing yourself. If Jesus Christ is the Word of God, we can say that in him God is expressing himself; that what is within this mysterious God, who is behind and beyond all things, finds expression in Jesus Christ the Son of God. The Word of God is God's self-expression. We might say that he is the very image of the Father (Colossians 1:15).

That leads us to another thing about words: they communicate. They take what is in my mind and heart and communicate it into yours. If Jesus Christ is the Word of God, he is God communicating God's own self, in order to unlock the mystery of who he is. Because Christ is God's Son, we know that there is a Father, of whom Christ is the image and likeness, a Father who wants to penetrate the darkness and make himself known to us. In Jesus Christ we see the Father.

Those who have seen the Son have seen the Father (John 14:9). Jesus Christ is the Word of the Father. In Jesus, the invisible is made visible. Notice again the words: 'the Word became flesh and lived among us'. In Jesus Christ, the language of eternity is translated into the language of time. God's eternal Word becomes flesh and is clothed in the kind of humanity that you and I can recognise and understand. We cannot speak God's language, so God comes to us speaking in our own. Jesus Christ is the great translator and the great translation of the living God, God's cross-cultural communication. For this reason John goes on to say, in today's passage, 'No one has ever seen God. It is God the only Son, who is close to the Father's heart, who has made him known' (v. 18). This is why we can say that he is the key that unlocks the secrets of God. This is why we should listen to him. This is where our journey must begin.

The Christ who is eternal

In the beginning was the Word, and the Word was with God, and the Word was God. He was in the beginning with God (vv. 1–2).

Our first journey is the journey of discovery. We are seeking to understand who Christ is in his fullness, in order that we may be fully devoted to him. If Christ is the key that unlocks the mystery of God's own being, this can only be because there is a way in which he shares God's being as God. According to our key verse, this means that he was 'in the beginning with God', and he 'was God'. We have to debate what this means. To be with God 'in the beginning' surely refers to the beginning of creation (Genesis 1:1). When space and time were summoned into being, the Word was already there, preceding it all. He was preceding it all because whatever God is, the Word also was. As we saw in yesterday's reading, John asserts that the Word who 'was' then 'became' flesh (v. 14). Something momentous and world-transforming happened: Christ became something he had not previously been—a part of the creation, sharing creation's finite limits and vulnerability, which is what 'flesh' implies.

Before we can make journeys of discovery or devotion, we need to see that Christ has first made his own journey from eternity into time. This clearly marks him out from any other human being. Human lives begin when they are conceived in the womb, but Christ is different. Christ 'was' before ever he was conceived in the womb. In the human being known as Jesus of Nazareth, the Word of God—who has been from the beginning, from eternity, who was with God and was God—has found expression and become incarnate. This means that the Word of God pre-existed the human person called Jesus of Nazareth, became identical with him in the incarnation and in this way became the Christ of God, who is God's saving gift to us.

In all of this, there is certainly a great deal that needs to be understood! Although, for many of us, these may be familiar truths, they can never stop being utterly astonishing ones. To say that Christ shares in eternity turns out to be a matter of the utmost importance. There are those who have tried to explain the importance of Jesus by saying that he was a human being especially favoured by God, even one who had been adopted by God to share in a special divine status. Others have thought that Jesus was created by God as the first and highest of God's works, a kind of angelic or semi-divine figure (although to be 'semi' divine would seem to be a contradiction in terms). But none of these attempts to honour Jesus really work. They succeed only in making Jesus less than the one he actually is, for underlying these apparently difficult patterns of thought there is one massive existential question: is Jesus Christ a human being to be revered and honoured only, or is the Word of God manifest in the flesh to be *worshipped*?

According to the Hebrew Scriptures, which Christians accept as the Old Testament, there is only one God, and that one God alone is to be worshipped (Deuteronomy 5:7; 6:4–5). To worship Christ, if he did not share in the divine being, would be wrong. It might be quite proper to honour and revere him, but certainly not to bow before him in worship, to call him 'my Lord and my God' (John 20:28) and give him divine honour and praise. Yet this is exactly what we find that the first

Christians did, and this is what the visions of the book of Revelation inspire Christians of all generations to do. Here, the Lamb of God (who is also the Word of God known as Jesus Christ) shares both the throne of God and the worship of God as 'every creature in heaven and on earth and under the earth and in the sea' says, 'To the one seated on the throne and to the Lamb be blessing and honour and glory and might for ever and ever!' (Revelation 5:13).

Jesus Christ is the key that unlocks the mystery of God

The eternity of the Christ is actually a quality associated with his deity, his sharing in the divine nature. It turns out to be a key assertion about the person of Christ. God is eternal; Christ is God; therefore Christ shares in eternity. To put it the other way round, Christ is eternal; eternity is a quality of God; therefore Christ is God. To make this claim is not abstract theology but a statement about something that is of the greatest importance to Christians and must be allowed to shape their lives. As we have already noted, without this statement it would not be appropriate for Christians to worship Christ. Yet this is exactly what they do whenever they pronounce the Gloria: 'Glory to the Father, and to the Son, and to the Holy Spirit, as it was in the beginning, is now and shall be for ever. Amen.'

Jesus Christ is the key that unlocks the mystery of God. We can add to that another belief: because he unlocks the mystery of God, he is also able to unlock the mystery of our own lives. He enables us to see ourselves within the framework of ultimate reality or of eternity. It is out of the mystery of eternity that Christ has come, giving a meaning to time. Everybody lives for something. The most thoughtful people know what they most value. It has been said that, strictly speaking, there is no such thing as a 'godless' man or woman. Everybody has something that they regard as their object of ultimate devotion, even if it may not be worthy of the name. It is important that whatever we live for is really worth the love and devotion we bring to it; otherwise we ourselves become diminished. We come to resemble whatever it is that we most honour. For Christians, to honour Christ is to root ourselves in someone who is of eternal value and significance, someone who is worthy, and that can only do us good.

To order a copy of this book, please turn to the order form on page 159.

Please note our subscription rates 2011–2012. From the May 2011 issue, the new subscription rates will be:

Individual subscriptions covering 3 issues for under 5 copies, payable in advance (including postage and packing):

	UK	SURFACE	AIRMAIL
GUIDELINES each set of 3 p.a.	£14.70	£16.50	£19.95
GUIDELINES 3-year sub i.e. 9 issues	£36.90	N/A	N/A
GUIDELINES pdf download (each set of 3 p.a.)	£11.70		

Group subscriptions covering 3 issues for 5 copies or more, sent to ONE address (post free):

GUIDELINES	£11.70 each set of 3 p.a.

Please note that the annual billing period for Group Subscriptions runs from 1 May to 30 April.

Copies of the notes may also be obtained from Christian bookshops:

GUIDELINES	£3.90 each copy

Visit www.biblereadingnotes.org.uk for information about our other Bible reading notes and Apple apps for iPhone and iPod touch.

As a Christian charity, BRF is involved in five distinct yet complementary areas.

- **BRF** (www.brf.org.uk) resources adults for their spiritual journey through Bible reading notes, books, and a programme of quiet days and teaching days. BRF also provides the infrastructure that supports our other four specialist ministries.
- **Foundations21** (www.foundations21.org.uk) provides flexible and innovative ways for individuals and groups to explore their Christian faith and discipleship through a multimedia internet-based resource.
- **Messy Church**, led by Lucy Moore (www.messychurch.org.uk), enables churches all over the UK (and increasingly abroad) to reach children and adults beyond the fringes of the church .
- **Barnabas in Churches** (www.barnabasinchurches.org.uk) helps churches to support, resource and develop their children's ministry with the under-11s more effectively.
- **Barnabas in Schools** (www.barnabasinschools.org.uk) enables primary school children and teachers to explore Christianity creatively and bring the Bible alive within RE and Collective Worship.

At the heart of BRF's ministry is a desire to equip adults and children for Christian living—helping them to read and understand the Bible, to explore prayer and to grow as disciples of Jesus. We need your help to make a real impact on the local church, local schools and the wider community.

- You could support BRF's ministry with a donation or standing order (using the response form overleaf).
- You could consider making a bequest to BRF in your will.
- You could encourage your church to support BRF as part of your church's giving to home mission—perhaps focusing on a specific area of our ministry, or a particular member of our Barnabas team.
- Most important of all, you could support BRF with your prayers.

If you would like to discuss how a specific gift or bequest could be used in the development of our ministry, please phone 01865 319700 or email enquiries@brf.org.uk.

Whatever you can do or give, we thank you for your support.

BRF MINISTRY APPEAL RESPONSE FORM

Name _____

Address _____

_____ Postcode _____

Telephone _____ Email _____

Gift Aid Declaration

❑ I am a UK taxpayer. I want BRF to treat as Gift Aid Donations all donations I make
from 6 April 2000 until I notify you otherwise.

Signature _____ Date _____

❑ I would like to support BRF's ministry with a regular donation by standing order

Standing Order – Banker's Order

To the Manager, Name of Bank/Building Society

Address _____

_____ Postcode _____

Sort Code _____ Account Name _____

Account No _____

Please pay Royal Bank of Scotland plc, Drummonds, 49 Charing Cross,
London SW1A 2DX (Sort Code 16-00-38), for the account of BRF A/C No. 00774151

The sum of _____ pounds on ___ /___ /___ (insert date) and thereafter the same
amount on the same day of each month annually until further notice.

Signature _____ Date _____

Single donation

❑ I enclose my cheque/credit card/Switch card details for a donation of
£5 £10 £25 £50 £100 £250 (other) £ _____ to support BRF's ministry

Card no. | | | | | | | | | | | | | | | | | |

Expires | | | | | Security code | | | |

Issue no. (Switch only) | | | |

Signature _____ Date _____

❑ Please send me information about making a bequest to BRF in my will.

Please detach and send this completed form to: Richard Fisher, BRF,
15 The Chambers, Vineyard, Abingdon OX14 3FE. BRF is a Registered Charity (No.233280)

❏ I would like to take out a subscription myself:

Your name _____

Your address _____

_____ Postcode _____

Tel _____ Email _____

Please send *Guidelines* beginning with the May 2011 / September 2011 / January 2012 issue: (delete as applicable)

(please tick box)	UK	SURFACE	AIR MAIL
GUIDELINES	❏ £14.70	❏ £16.50	❏ £19.95
GUIDELINES 3-year sub	❏ £36.90		
GUIDELINES pdf download	❏ £11.70 (UK and overseas)		

❏ I would like to give a gift subscription (please complete both name and address sections above and below):

Gift subscription name _____

Gift subscription address _____

_____ Postcode _____

Gift message (20 words max. or include your own gift card for the recipient)

_____

_____

Please send *Guidelines* beginning with the May 2011 / September 2011 / January 2012 issue: (delete as applicable)

(please tick box)	UK	SURFACE	AIR MAIL
GUIDELINES	❏ £14.70	❏ £16.50	❏ £19.95
GUIDELINES 3-year sub	❏ £36.90		
GUIDELINES pdf download	❏ £11.70 (UK and overseas)		

Please complete your payment details overleaf.

SUBSCRIPTION PAYMENT DETAILS

Please complete the payment details below and send with appropriate payment and completed Subscriptions order form to:

BRF, 15 The Chambers, Vineyard, Abingdon OX14 3FE

Total enclosed £ _____ (cheques should be made payable to 'BRF')

Please charge my Visa ❏ Mastercard ❏ Switch card ❏ with £ _____

Card no: | | | | | | | | | | | | | | | | | | |

Expires | | | | Security code | | |

Issue no (Switch only) | | | |

Signature (essential if paying by credit/Switch) _____

❏ Please do not send me further information about BRF publications.

BRF is a Registered Charity

GL 0111

BRF PUBLICATIONS ORDER FORM

Please ensure that you complete and send off both sides of this order form.
Please send me the following book(s):

		Quantity	Price	Total
704 4	Jesus Christ—the Alpha & the Omega (N.G. Wright)	_____	£7.99	_____
757 0	Celebrating the King James Version (R. Boulding)	_____	£9.99	_____
823 2	Meditating with Scripture: John's Gospel (E. Bosetti)	_____	£7.99	_____
788 4	The Promise of Easter (F. Dorrell)	_____	£4.99	_____
503 3	Messy Church (L. Moore)	_____	£8.99	_____
602 3	Messy Church 2 (L. Moore)	_____	£8.99	_____
852 2	The People's Bible (M. Payne)	_____	£5.99	_____
191 2	PBC: Matthew (J. Proctor)	_____	£8.99	_____
046 5	PBC: Mark (D. France)	_____	£8.99	_____
027 4	PBC: Luke (H. Wansbrough)	_____	£8.99	_____
850 8	PBC: John (R.A. Burridge)	_____	£8.99	_____
216 2	PBC: Acts (L. Alexander)	_____	£8.99	_____
850 8	PBC: Romans (J. Dunn)	_____	£8.99	_____
122 6	PBC: 1 Corinthians (J. Murphy-O'Connor)	_____	£8.99	_____
073 1	PBC: 2 Corinthians (Aída Besançon Spencer)	_____	£8.99	_____

Total cost of books £ _____

Donation £ _____

Postage and packing £ _____

TOTAL £ _____

POSTAGE AND PACKING CHARGES				
order value	UK	Europe	Surface	Air Mail
£7.00 & under	£1.25	£3.00	£3.50	£5.50
£7.01–£30.00	£2.25	£5.50	£6.50	£10.00
Over £30.00	free	prices on request		

For more information about new books and special offers, visit www.brfonline.org.uk.

See over for payment details.

All prices are correct at time of going to press, are subject to the prevailing rate of VAT and may be subject to change without prior warning.

WAYS TO ORDER BRF RESOURCES

Christian bookshops: All good Christian bookshops stock BRF publications. For your nearest stockist, please contact BRF.

Telephone: The BRF office is open between 09.15 and 17.30. To place your order, phone 01865 319700; fax 01865 319701.

Web: Visit www.brfonline.org.uk

By post: Please complete the payment details below and send with appropriate payment and completed order form to:

BRF, 15 The Chambers, Vineyard, Abingdon OX14 3FE

Name _____

Address _____

_____ Postcode _____

Telephone _____

Email _____

Total enclosed £ _____ (cheques should be made payable to 'BRF')

Please charge my Visa ❑ Mastercard ❑ Switch card ❑ with £ _____

Card no: | | | | | | | | | | | | | | | | | | | |

Expires | | | | Security code | | |

Issue no (Switch only) | | | |

~ (essential if paying by credit/Switch) _____

send me further information about BRF publications.

BRF is a Registered Charity

659

GL 0111